Columbia University Lectures

WORLD ORGANIZATION AS AFFECTED BY
THE NATURE OF THE MODERN STATE

THE CARPENTIER LECTURES

1910–1911

By the Same Author

A History of Diplomacy in the International Development of Europe

Vol. I — The Struggle for Universal Empire. With five Colored Maps, Chronological Tables of Emperors, Popes, and Rulers; Lists of Treaties and other Public Acts, and Index. Pp. xxiii + 481. $5.00 net.

Vol. II — The Establishment of Territorial Sovereignty. With four Colored Maps, Tables, etc., and Index. Pp. xxiv + 688. $5.00 net.

THIS work presents a consecutive account of the international development of Europe from its organization under the Roman Empire. Beginning with civilized Europe as a united community, it traces its transformation through the successive phases of its history, including its expansion into new territory, the formation of separate national states, the establishment of an international system of law and intercourse, and the progress of that system through the negotiation of treaties and the application of principles of jurisprudence. It thus aims to consider the political system of Europe as a whole in a manner similar to that in which the constitutional history of a single state considers that of a particular political community.

From the *American Historical Review* : —

"The industry, the insight, and the thoroughness with which . . . he has acquainted himself, as to all points cardinal to his theme, with the best and latest in the teeming literature of the subject, are striking."

COLUMBIA UNIVERSITY PRESS SALES AGENTS

NEW YORK: Lemcke & Buechner
30–32 West 27th Street

LONDON: Henry Frowde
Amen Corner, E.C.

TORONTO: Henry Frowde
25 Richmond Street, W.

COLUMBIA UNIVERSITY LECTURES

WORLD ORGANIZATION

AS AFFECTED BY THE NATURE OF THE MODERN STATE

BY

DAVID JAYNE HILL

New York
THE COLUMBIA UNIVERSITY PRESS
1911

All rights reserved

COPYRIGHT, 1911,
BY THE COLUMBIA UNIVERSITY PRESS.

Set up and electrotyped. Published May, 1911.

Aug 3, 1943
J. Hist.

320.15
H551w

Norwood Press
J. S. Cushing Co. — Berwick & Smith Co.
Norwood, Mass., U.S.A.

PREFACE

THE text of this book consists of eight lectures delivered before the Columbia University, on the Carpentier Foundation, in March, 1911.

The views expressed are strictly personal, and involve no responsibility on the part of anyone except the author.

It hardly needs to be stated, that there is no pretence of anything like a systematic presentation of a theory of the State, either as to its origin or its nature, considered in a general or abstract sense. Only certain aspects of the Modern State, as it exists, have been considered; and these merely with the purpose of showing the way in which the problem of a wider juristic organization is affected by its nature and development.

In citing the views of jurists and writers on International Law, no attempt has been made to set forth their doctrines or theories with completeness. They have been quoted or referred to solely for the purpose of explaining or illustrating the line of thought here followed, and their systems as a whole should be studied in their own works or in the explicit and symmetrical expositions of them to be found in the writings of those who have attempted to interpret their meaning.

The main idea of these lectures, reinforced from several different points of view, is the growth of jural consciousness among all civilized nations, and its embodiment in the Modern State; — a phenomenon which is believed to have an important bearing upon international life and intercourse.

DAVID JAYNE HILL.

APRIL, 1911.

CONTENTS

LECTURE	PAGE
I. THE STATE AS AN EMBODIMENT OF LAW	1
Early Aspirations after the Reign of Law	2
Law Inherent in Society	4
Natural, Moral, and Jural Laws	5
The Modern State as the Protagonist of Law	8
The Achievements of Organized Force under Law	10
The Danger of the Omnipotence of the State	12
The Pretension of Supremacy to Law	13
The Condition of International Anarchy	15
The Genesis and Development of the State	15
Machiavelli's Theory of Absolutism	17
Bodin's Conception of Sovereignty	19
The Place of the State in the Juristic Order	22
II. THE STATE AS A JURISTIC PERSON	26
The Althusian Postulate of Inherent Rights	27
Grotius' Idea of Law Imposed by Nature	30
Pufendorf's Idea of the State as a Moral Person	33
The State Considered as a Person	36
The Relation of the State to Moral Law	39
The Inadequacy of Moral Law for the State	42
The Alleged Exemption of the State from Morality	44
The Necessary Interpretation of Moral Law	45
The Relation of a Statesman to the Morality of Public Policies	47
Public and Private Morality	49
III. THE STATE AS A PROMOTER OF GENERAL WELFARE	53
The Duty of the State to its Constituents	53
The State and its Government	55
The Defence of National Interests	57
The Development of a National Conscience	59
Government as the Curator of the State	61

CONTENTS

LECTURE		PAGE
	The Function of Diplomacy	62
	Dangers Arising from Advantages *in Posse*	64
	Duties of the State as a Juristic Entity	65
	The Alleged Essential Egoism of the State	67
	The Classic Maxims of Diplomacy	69
	The New Element in the Modern State	72
	The Need of Guarantees of Justice	74
IV.	THE STATE AS A MEMBER OF A SOCIETY	77
	The Unifying Influence of the Church	78
	Suarez' Recognition of the Society of States	81
	The Outlawry of the Stranger in Primitive Times	83
	The Gradual Recognition of the Stranger's Rights	85
	The Development of Self-consciousness in the Society of States	87
	The Thirty Years' War and the Peace of Westphalia	91
	The Significance of the Peace of Westphalia	93
	The Influence of New Theories of Government upon the Society of States	95
	The Effect of Locke's Doctrine on the Conception of Sovereignty	98
	The Import of Locke's Theory for International Society	100
	The Mandate of Man to his Governments	102
V.	THE STATE AS A SUBJECT OF POSITIVE LAW	104
	What is Civilization?	104
	The State the Measure of Civilization	107
	The Essential Unity of Civilization	109
	The Opposition of "Naturalists" and "Positivists"	111
	The Adherents of Grotius	113
	Wolf's Conception of the World-State	115
	The Rôle of Jurisprudence in Diplomacy	117
	The Nature and Authority of International Law	120
	The Proposed Codification of International Law	123
	The Contemporary Evolution of International Law	125
	The Subjection of the State to the Reign of Law	127
VI.	THE STATE AS A MEDIATOR OF GUARANTEES	130
	The Guarantees of International Equilibrium	131
	Inadequacy of the System of Equilibrium	133
	The Principle of Federation	135

CONTENTS

LECTURE		PAGE
	Impediments to General Federation	138
	The Limitations of Independence	139
	International Intervention and Supervision	140
	The Principle of Neutralization	142
	The Jural Relations of Independent States	144
	The Adaptability of the Modern State for Jural Guarantees	146
	The Limit and Basis of International Guarantees	148
VII.	THE STATE AS AN ARMED POWER	151
	The Value of Military Virtue	152
	The Rôle of Force in Civilization	154
	The Movement for Limiting Armaments	156
	The Attitude toward International Justice in the First Hague Conference	159
	The Triumph of the Juristic Idea in 1907	162
	The Juristic Conception not yet Organized	164
	The Warlike Maintenance of Peace	165
	The Peaceful Regulation of War	167
	The Judicial Organization of Peace	169
	Profit and Loss in War	172
	Is War "Inevitable"?	173
VIII.	THE STATE AS A JUSTICIABLE PERSON	175
	The Evolution of Organized Justice	175
	The Right of War	178
	The Fallacy of the Absolute Right of War	181
	The Principle of Inviolability	184
	The Responsibility of the State	186
	The Subordination of the State to Judicial Principles	188
	The Progress of International Justice	190
	The Limitation of the Employment of Armed Force	193
	The Establishment of International Courts	195
	The Demands for International Justice from the Business World	197
	Summary and Conclusion	199
INDEX		203

I

THE STATE AS AN EMBODIMENT OF LAW

IF we spread before us the map of Europe and the map of Africa, and imagine ourselves about to start upon a journey unattended, first in the one and then in the other of these continents, we cannot avoid the impression that our preparation in the two cases would have to be somewhat different. We might travel from one end of Europe to the other without carrying with us any means of self-defence, but we should hardly venture into the interior of Africa without being well provided with guns and ammunition.

The reason for this difference in our personal outfit would be the different social conditions in which we should find ourselves placed. In Europe, we should be in a land where the State has reached a high degree of perfection. In Africa, we should find ourselves, a great part of the time, among primitive tribes, where the State either does not exist, or exists in a very rudimentary form. In Europe, justice is so organized that we should everywhere enjoy the protection of law. In certain parts of Africa, we should be compelled to protect our lives and property against the attacks of savage men.

By "world organization" we understand the task of so uniting governments in the support of principles of justice as to apply them not only within the limits of the State but also between States.

There appear to be in the nature of the Modern Constitutional State new and hitherto unappreciated grounds for believing, that powerful social forces, which have in the past been working in isolation, are becoming so interrelated as to result in unity of action; for it must not be overlooked, that the problem of world organization is new only in its wider extension, and not in the conditions with which it has to deal. It is, in fact, simply the problem of the further development and more perfect coördination of forms of progress which have thus far marked the advance of public order in the world; and we might perhaps quite fairly describe it as the problem of general social evolution regarded from the point of view of jurisprudence.

EARLY ASPIRATIONS AFTER THE REIGN OF LAW

When we turn our attention to those lands which we call "civilized," where public security now prevails, we observe that this result has been obtained only through a long course of development. If we examine the subject in the light of history, we are impressed with the fact that the reign of law, and through it the establishment of public order, is among the most ancient and persistent of the aspirations of mankind. Repeatedly baffled in their endeavors to create a permanent condition of security, succeeding generations have returned with new ardor to the task; and it may be said, that the realization of this ideal has been the highest endeavor of all who at any time have most contributed to the progress of civilization.

It is not necessary for the purpose we have in mind to review even briefly the endeavors to realize this ideal. The Greeks attempted to embody it in more or less loosely associated city-states; the Romans to give it wider extension in the form of universal empire. The struggles that grew out of this last endeavor, under its political and spiritual forms, constituted for more than a thousand years the principal drama of European history, and their influence is still felt in every portion of the earth.

The postulates of the Roman imperial idea have never ceased, and perhaps never will cease, to command the respect of all intelligent men. The essential unity of mankind, the supremacy of law based upon reason, the solidarity of all human interests, and the effective organization of peace as a condition of human happiness, — these are some of the splendid conceptions which dominated the Roman mind and gave an inherent dignity to the idea of universal empire.

As obstacles to this magisterial theory of uniform law and central administration, there appeared in practice the passions, ambitions, and rivalries of leaders; the disparity of races; the spirit of local independence; the physical limitations of time and space to central control; and the conflict between the temporal and spiritual forms of obedience. As a consequence, every kind of universal authority eventually suffered a defeat; and universal law, founded solely upon abstract reason, — formal, impersonal, and logical by its essential nature, — was compelled to yield to impulse, interest, self-sufficiency, and experiment, working themselves out in their own independent way under local conditions.

Had the imperial idea triumphed, there would be no problem of world organization. Mankind everywhere would be under one law and subject to one authority. But the imperial idea has failed in practice; and, having failed, must, therefore, be abandoned. It does not, however, follow that its postulates were false. We can only infer that they were wrongly applied, and it is evident in what way the application was erroneous. Reason, the common possession of all men, was not the monopoly of one man or of one people. Being the property of all, its manifestations must be sought in the consciousness and the experience of all; and its whole rich content can be known only through the diversity of its revelations.

LAW INHERENT IN SOCIETY

It is not then abstract reason which furnishes the basis of law and the foundations of existing public order. It is rather reason in its concrete disclosures, in its specific applications, as the guide of practical life in the whole volume of human experience. This is the interpretation of authority that has constructed the Modern State, as distinguished from the imperial idea. This form of polity is primarily local, concrete, and experimental. It rises out of the actual needs of men. Instead of receiving law from a philosopher's study, or a transcendental source claiming divine authority, or from the throne of a Caesar, it is accepted as a necessity arising from the nature and social needs of men. Every human individual stands in a relation to nature. He is a child, an embodiment, of nature. He is formed of its elements, he is charged with its energies, he is controlled by its laws. He cannot separate himself from it, for nature is the great law-giver. He must renew his body from the soil, he must breathe the air, he must provide against the changing seasons; or he cannot exist. In a similar manner, he is related to his kind. He is one of a series; ancestry stands behind him, and posterity will follow after him. He is also one of a group, — brother and sister, fellow and neighbor, friend or enemy. He cannot wholly sunder himself from these. Isolation means death, and his whole existence depends upon a living relation to this human environment.

What then results from these necessary relations? The individual must live in some kind of harmony with these natural and social conditions. He must draw his resources from them, and he must give back in return from his store of strength and possessions. In so far as he is necessarily a receiver, he has *rights*, — personal claims upon the conditions of existence and self-development. In so far as he must give back in return, he has *duties*, — obligations to fulfil. These opposite sides of personal relation are bound together by a bond which cannot be broken without the repudiation of practical reason. There is no physical bond. A man may always receive, and never contribute, if the community will permit him to do so. But there is a rational bond. If he can give a reason why he should receive, that in itself constitutes a reason why he should give back, if he be able. In brief, if he "ought" to receive, he "ought" also to contribute. Rights and duties are only opposite sides of the same relation, the essential properties of personality.

From this it follows that wherever there is society there is law; that is, there are general rules of conduct by which rights and duties may be determined and organized. And here we need to distinguish with great care, for there is perhaps in the whole range of human concepts no other so persistently confused and so fertile in fallacies as the idea of "law."

NATURAL, MORAL, AND JURAL LAWS

It may, therefore, be useful to recall very clearly the difference between three entirely distinct classes of laws, having no quality in common, except a general relation to conduct; yet all designated by the same word.

1. The phenomena of nature occur in accordance with certain invariable modes of procedure, or universal formulas of sequence and coexistence. These are *natural* laws in the scientific sense, which we may regard or disregard, but can never in any proper sense violate; because they cannot be affected by our conduct, which makes no change in nature, although it may determine what may happen to ourselves. Such general statements of universal facts are expository of the conditions of existence; as, for example, the law of gravitation, which we cannot ignore without bodily harm. Our whole existence is regulated by such laws, without regard to our consent, and our interest in them arises from the fact that knowledge of them discloses to us the conditions upon which our lives depend.

2. In the relations of human beings to one another, there are certain rules of conduct, — not indeed invariably observed, — which so affect the harmony of our existence and our consciousness of obligation that, whether enforced or not, we feel that they justly claim our respect and obedience. They relate not only to our outward acts but to our dispositions of mind and heart also, claiming authority over our inner life, and giving rise to the distinction between "virtue" on the one hand and "vice" on the other. These are *moral* laws, having their basis in the constitution of human nature; but not generalizations of fact, like the natural laws just described. They are rather directions for conduct; imperative as admonitions but not compulsory in effect, serving as guides on the pathway to personal and social development, and pointing the road to nobility of character and the higher harmonies of human association. These laws say to us: "Thou shalt not covet thy neighbor's goods;" "Thou shalt not bear false witness against thy neighbor;" or, in more positive form:

"Thou shalt love thy neighbor as thyself." They cover the whole realm of conduct, including its sources in disposition and tendency, as well as intention. Obedience or disobedience are left to our choice, but they are not without their consequences, even though these are not always in the form of outward penalties. The rain falls alike on the just and on the unjust; but justice, charity, truthfulness, forbearance, and all other virtues nevertheless bear their fruits. These consequences follow natural and inevitable lines of growth or decay in us. They modify character and determine destiny; leaving us on the one hand elevated and ennobled, on the other debased and degraded. They reveal to us our true and just position in the scale of being, according to the dominant traits of our natures and our deeds.

3. There is another class of rules of action, not so broad and general in their scope as moral laws, but even more definite in their expression. There are certain forms of conduct and abstention so necessary to the well-being of society that they have to be insisted upon for the security of existence. No form of human association, even the most theocratic, can enforce the entire moral code; for the reason that the dispositions and intentions to which moral laws apply are inaccessible to every form of outward compulsion. But there are certain rights and duties so manifestly essential to the existence and development of the individual and the community that some recognition of them is necessary in every form of society, and these must be enforced by public authority. Such rules as are needful for this purpose, which vary in different stages of social complexity, dealing with essential rights of person and property and enforced by fixed penalties, may be called *jural* laws. If men universally rendered implicit obedience to the precepts of morality, jural laws would be superfluous;

but no community of men has ever been able to trust entirely to the goodness of its members, without imposing mandatory rules of conduct enforced by punishment when they were not respected. These laws may consist in unrecorded customs, in the decrees of personal rulers, or in self-protective statutes prescribed by the will of the people; but, in some form, jural laws, as well as moral laws, exist wherever society exists. Without regard to traditions, theories, or systems, they arise spontaneously and inevitably, because without them human rights, which are the vital content of human existence, would possess no security.

THE MODERN STATE THE EMBODIMENT AND PROTAGONIST OF LAW

It seems at times as if the failure of the imperial idea had been more than compensated for by the fact that men in so many different fields have been forced back upon the inherent necessities of nature and society; and, as it were, compelled by the exercise of their own faculties to work out the problem of their legal protection in the light of their own particular needs. Instead of being broken into subjection by the chariot wheels of imperial conquest and driven under the yoke of a universal law conceived as a deduction from abstract right, the nations have been able to build up their own jural conceptions for themselves; and thus finally to emerge into a common arena of juristic apprehension, to which each has arrived in its own way, but with a deep sense of the reality of the jural idea.

It is true, no doubt, that Roman Law, whose conquests were far more extensive and enduring than those of the Roman legions, has exercised a mighty influence upon the whole of continental Europe, and far beyond its borders; but this influence is due more to the inherent soundness of the Roman conceptions of right than to any extraneous circumstance.

As a consequence, the Modern State, notwithstanding the imperishable community that Rome through its institutions impressed upon the whole of civilization, is essentially a local institution. In this it has the advantage of being rooted deeply in the soil which in each case has produced it; and can, nowhere in Europe at least, be regarded as an importation. Whatever it may be in its composite structure, and it undoubtedly contains exotic elements, it is not a system produced either by conquest or by abstract reasoning. It is essentially territorial. It may spread its administration over the breadth of a continent and regulate by its laws the lives of scores of millions of men, but it has still a local jurisdiction, interpreting the needs of a particular population; and, however remote from the centre its boundaries may be, it has definite frontiers; while beyond these are other States, equally local, equally independent, and with no permanent organic connection between them. They are as entirely separate, and as complete in their autonomy as a group of adjacent planets would be, with no bond of unity between them except coexistence in space.

But when we ask ourselves, "What is there in common between these States?" we are compelled to answer, "It is their jural consciousness, their resolution to perfect their condition through their laws." And if we ask, "What is most modern in them, what most distinguishes their present from their past?" we must again answer, "It is their jural consciousness." The Modern State has become, through its own internal development, the embodiment and protagonist of jural law as the security for human rights.

Thus conceived, the State is entitled to our highest respect and perfect loyalty, as the greatest of human institutions. It stands before us as the incorporation of justice, or of the nearest approach to justice which our limitations permit us to attain. It aims, in harmony with natural conditions as revealed to us by science, progressively to translate into jural forms as much of the content of the moral law as is consistent with individual liberty; and limits liberty only when and where it becomes injurious to others. Theoretically at least, the State affords the strongest citadel for our rights, and the most hopeful medium for the realization of our ideals of perfect equity. If it is imperfect, it is because we who shape its destinies are imperfect. It should eventually embody the best thought and the highest resolutions of the human race.

There is then created within us by the contemplation of the nature of the State, a conviction that, through its agency, there may be found a solution to the problem of world organization, which at first may have appeared so far beyond the reach of human power. Certainly, if this enterprise is ever to succeed, it must be effected by the instrumentality of the State; or rather by the associated action of all civilized States, through the help of their collective strength, and under the guidance of their collective wisdom.

THE ACHIEVEMENTS OF ORGANIZED FORCE UNDER LAW

We must first of all recognize the fact, that over very much of the earth's surface, on all the continents and in the greater groups of islands, the State is firmly established; and jural law, with its accessories of physical protection, even now prevails. Not only so, but by the combined efforts of civilized nations piracy has been driven from the seas and oceans, and the advance of trade and colonization, supported by governmental safeguards, has left only a few geographical areas where it is not safe for civilized men to penetrate.

This achievement has been rendered possible by the effective arming of responsible public powers, and especially by the mobility afforded to the means of exercising their authority through the development of modern navies.

Regarded from this point of view, the immense advantages secured by the ability to protect life and property and enforce respect for rights and interests in regions where the State has no established authority fully justify a great interest in power upon the sea. When intended as an effectual means for the maintenance of order in turbulent portions of the earth, or as a necessary instrument for the defence of exposed territories, no reasonable man can object to the augmentation of the power of the State in this direction. When needed for these purposes, a powerful navy is the most trustworthy auxiliary of law and order. When, on the other hand, it is considered what large demands naval armaments are making upon the resources of certain peoples, what a terrific menace to life and property these agents of destruction would be if devoted to evil purposes, and how exposed governments are to the incalculable' contingencies of popular impulse in moments of excitement, it is of the highest importance to the welfare of mankind that these vast energies should be employed only in strict accordance with the principles of equity, and that effective guarantees should be given that they will not be misused. In order to fulfil its mission as the guardian of human rights and the protagonist of law, the State must be entrusted with sufficient organized force to repress wrongdoing and maintain in all emergencies public order; but we must not overlook the fact, that we have invested it with powers vastly more enormous than it has ever before possessed.

THE DANGER OF THE OMNIPOTENCE OF THE STATE

There is, without doubt, a great danger in the omnipotence of the State. During the greater part of human history, government has been arbitrary; and has enshrouded its right to be so in some mysterious halo of sanctity. The helplessness, dependence, and ignorance of men have rendered them powerless to resist its assumptions. Looking up to it as the highest earthly authority, they have been taught to regard it as possessing a divine prerogative. It has usually, and not unnaturally, entrenched its pretensions in what was most sacred in their sentiments and consciences, and when it could not dominate them by superior force it has rendered them passive through an appeal to their religious obligations.

In this respect there has been a great change. The State can no longer speak and act irresponsibly in the name of the deity, or clothe itself in the garb of superhuman attributes or divine supremacy. In modern times, men have come to understand that government is necessary to their well-being, and exists for their safety and happiness; but that it possesses no attributes not derived from their collective will and purposes.

The time has gone by for civilized nations when predatory warfare was looked upon as a form of enterprise to which public powers might be rightly applied. There is probably no responsible statesman in any civilized country who would publicly propose a war of conquest and subjugation for the sake of the spoils, either in the form of booty or territory;

and there is no civilized nation that would seriously contemplate such a policy. Certainly there is none that would openly avow it. Yet every nation wishes to be as a strong man armed. Every responsible government is anxious to incur no blame for delinquency in preparing for the defence of the national interests wherever they may be endangered, and this is the ground upon which the vast expenditures for military purposes are urged and justified in every parliament. Everywhere the plea for armament is the national defence.

Looking at the subject from the point of view of each particular nation, it would be difficult to find fault with this attitude; yet, regarded from a more general point of view, it is evident that the expense for military purposes is often excessive, that every excess in this direction stimulates others, and that the tendency of this passion for armament is to excite universal suspicion, create unnecessary alarm, and produce a situation which is artificial, unreasonable, and extremely dangerous.

It is not just, however, to argue that the course pursued is absurd, because it would be ridiculous for individuals in a peaceable community to arm themselves; for the duty of maintaining the public defence is a specific obligation assumed by the State, and if it failed to make adequate provision for security, it would be delinquent in the exercise of one of the most important of public functions.

THE PRETENSION OF SUPREMACY TO LAW

Nor is it fair for one power to accuse another of evil purposes, because it desires to be strong. The peril to peace and to peaceful interests does not lie in the fact that the State is strong. There would be far greater peril if it were notably weak; for then it could not fulfil its obligations, would invite interference, and thereby perhaps endanger its existence. The real peril lies in the pretension of the State that it may employ force, not only in defending its interests from attack, but in any manner it may see fit, without regard to principles of law or forms of judicial procedure. That which justifies thoughtful men in dreading the growth of armaments, and the resulting omnipotence of the State, is not that the State is strong, but its refusal to give guarantees that it will always be just.

The fundamental imperfection in the existing order of things is not the presence of armaments, even though they may be excessive; nor is the chief remedy to be found in any scheme of disarmament. That excess is merely a symptom, not a cause, of danger. We do not require that all individuals in society shall be of equal strength, nor that one man shall reduce his strength in the interest of other men. What we require is, that all men, whatever their size or strength may be, shall recognize and obey the law; and every good citizen voluntarily submits himself to it.

But it is not so with States. They continue to claim the right, which is subversive of the whole conception of right, to act as they see fit. Existing, as they do, for the protection of rights, they refuse to enter into a definite, binding jural system. They employ the term "sovereignty" for a double purpose. They use it as a basis of authority, and as a ground for exemption. As regards their right to command obedience, they profess to be the embodiment of law; but as regards their mutual obligations, they assert their supremacy to law. They claim the privilege of defining their own rights, but they refuse to assume or to permit any power to impose upon them corresponding duties. They are a law unto themselves.

THE CONDITION OF INTERNATIONAL ANARCHY

The condition of the world, from an international point of view, has long been one of polite anarchy. There is an international etiquette, there are forms of courtesy, there are venerable customs, there are certain limited engagements under the seal of solemn conventions, and there are recognized principles of international ethics; but, none the less, juristically speaking, there exists a condition of anarchy. Three centuries ago, there were four or five hundred potentates claiming the right to make war upon whom, and for whatever reason, it was their "good pleasure" to make it. This "right" involved the privilege of killing inoffensive populations, of capturing and sacking cities, and of annexing territories. The same kind of "right" is to-day confined to some fifty or sixty "Sovereign Powers"; but it rests upon the same foundation, and includes the same freedom from restraint.

What is the foundation upon which this alleged "right" rests?

It rests upon the attribute of "sovereignty"; that is to say, the property of supremacy to law.

The State is "sovereign," in the sense that its authority is absolute and supreme. It knows no superior.

Like many another inheritance from the past, this conception of "sovereignty" runs through our whole system of public law, permeates judicial decisions, and furnishes the favorite basis for the theory of the State.

THE GENESIS AND DEVELOPMENT OF THE STATE

Happily, we are acquainted with the genesis and development of the State as it exists, for it is of comparatively recent origin. In the Middle Ages, in its modern sense, it had no existence. Society in the greater part of Europe subsisted under two forms: the Church and the Empire, theoretically correlated, and each claiming universal sway. Locally, the peoples were ruled by their princes, secular and spiritual; who, under the gradations of the feudal system and the ecclesiastical hierarchy, formed a double series of related obediences. Each prince had his *état*, his *status*, which implied some kind of authority; but the State in its modern sense had no being. With the formation of the national monarchies, the sovereigns, aided by the people in crushing out the more immediate and therefore more oppressive feudatories, gradually assumed the authority within their realms, established their law-courts, formed their national armies, and offered a better administration and a more sure protection against wrong and invasion. Through the development of parliaments, assemblies, and finally formal constitutions, public authority became less personal and more institutional and thus created the State in its modern sense.

It is important to note, that, in the process of its evolution, the State has been chiefly the product of will, only dimly guided by intelligence. Neither natural geographic boundaries, nor racial affinities, nor linguistic community have determined its formation. Its primal cause was dynastic interest supported by military force. Only in very recent times has theory had any influence upon the constitution of the State. It sprang from more or less accidental cohesions, in which marriage and the combination of inheritances played a large rôle, and intelligent constructive design comparatively little.

Thus came into being certain definite complexes of associated populations, presided over by the more powerful princes through successful competition with the less powerful, dwelling within given territorial areas more or less fortuitously or arbitrarily combined, and delimited by the like growth of rival neighbors. Within these areas, through the coöperation of dynastic authority and the community of historic memories created by participation in a common cause of defence, development, and expansion, the national units of Europe have been formed. In the contemporary States and their colonial offspring the dynastic beginnings have in part been obscured by their later development, but traces of these still remain in the symbolism that gives color to the modern conception of the State and its attributes. Among these is that of "sovereignty," an idea formed by abstracting the qualities formerly possessed by a sovereign ruler placed by virtue of his position above the law, since he was regarded as its source. Invested with all the qualities of the Roman *imperium* by the students of the ancient imperial law of Rome, the "sovereign" stood apart, elevated above the mass, supreme and absolute, until modern constitutionalism divested him of these potentialities and transferred them to the State, to which they are still attributed.

MACHIAVELLI'S THEORY OF ABSOLUTISM

If now we turn our attention from the concrete sovereign to the abstract attribute of sovereignty, we may trace in a few words the development of the theory which makes it the essence of the State.

The old Roman formula went little beyond the fact. It ran, "*Quidquid principi placuit legis habet vigorum,*" — whatever pleases the prince has the force of law. The advocates of absolutism managed to forget the qualification given by Justinian, "*Utpote quum lege regia populus ei et in eum suum imperium et potestatem conferat,*"[1] which even from an imperial point of view referred the origin of all law-making power to the people. The modern theorists have restored this qualification, and ascribe sovereignty to the people as a whole, — who in truth are very dimly conscious of it; — but it has never at any time been made quite clear how the people can bestow what they do not possess, namely, absolute supremacy, unlimited by law or obligation.

It is interesting to see how the theory of the State, which is manifestly a mere mental creation, subject to constant modification and development, is usually derived by a process of abstraction from some favorite form of actual government. The method of concrete observation possesses all the appearance of a scientific process because it proceeds by analysis and induction. Thus Machiavelli (1469–1527),[2] the first modern to make a real contribution to political science, takes his conception of the State from the successful monarchies of France and Spain, highly centralized unitary states and splendid examples of political perfection, in comparison with dismembered Italy, the victim of discord and anarchy. He sees the remedy in the tyranny of Cesare Borgia, the strong despot, imposing his will without regard to moral scruples. The State, creation of the Prince, is in his view essentially nonmoral. Any crime may be committed in its name. It knows no law higher than success. Mankind is totally depraved, and must by any means be beaten into order; and this can be done only by an unlimited will. Above the Prince there is

[1] The *Digest* of Justinian, I, 41; and Carlyle, *A History of Mediaeval Political Theory in the West*, Edinburgh, 1903, I, p. 70.

[2] *Il Principi*, Burd's edition, Oxford, 1891. See also the admirable discussion of Machiavelli's doctrines in Villari, *The Life and Time of Machiavelli*, London, 1898, II, pp. 89, 184.

THE STATE AS AN EMBODIMENT OF LAW

no authority to impose rules of action upon him. He is the possessor of sovereign power. Religion and morality may be useful instruments; but they are for him only agencies, not authorities. To the unity, strength, and growth of the State everything else must be sacrificed.

It is unfortunate, perhaps, that Machiavelli's philosophy became the classic of European statesmanship, but events gave it a high authority. The *raison d'état*, a principle that recognizes no *lex altior*, became the general rule of political action. It was the triumph of realism in government, and the consequent suppression for many centuries of those ideals which constitute the fertilizing element in political progress. What is worst of all is the persistence of Machiavelli's fundamental error that the essence of the State lies in some particular form of government; whereas the two conceptions are entirely distinct. The nature of the State is to be discovered in the *ends* for which it exists as an institution, while forms of government are to be judged according to their efficiency as *means* for accomplishing those ends. For Machiavelli the Prince was the State, not merely the agent for promoting the general welfare. For him, therefore, the Prince was supreme; not the servant of great human purposes, but the original source of all authority, above whom there was no law. It was a convenient doctrine for a creative period, but it sinks and obscures the purpose of the State in the supremacy of its ruler.

BODIN'S CONCEPTION OF SOVEREIGNTY

It is an interesting reflection that the world has been most deeply and permanently impressed by exceptional experiences. The remedy which Machiavelli sought for the political anguish of Italy remained the most persistent influence upon the political thought of Europe until another great convulsion evoked another great writing, which has since held its place with Machiavelli's "Prince."

The Wars of Religion of the latter half of the sixteenth century nearly accomplished the dismemberment of France. In an age of deep unrest, conspiracy, and private war, culminating in the horrors of St. Bartholomew's Day, men turned in despair to a rehabilitation of the State, and there was awakened a new interest in its nature and authority. Among the discussions of that time the most notable was the work of Jean Bodin (1530–1596), "De la République," published originally in French in 1576, translated by him into Latin in 1591, and destined to become for a long period the most celebrated classic on the nature of the State.[1]

It is the first work in which the conception of "sovereignty" is distinctly treated, and its author makes that idea the corner-stone of his entire system. What Bodin sought to produce was a reasoned exposition of a natural ground for regal omnipotence. It was necessary first of all to find a principle on which that idea could be logically based. It was not sufficient, therefore, merely to analyze the existing institution of monarchy; an abstract theory of the State must be supplied, founded on axioms of reason, which could serve as a new foundation for the monarch's throne.

In order that the reasoning might appeal to all men, Bodin placed in the title of his work the word "republic," the most generic term available for his purpose, and in laying the foundations of his system carefully avoided recommending any

---

[1] See also the expositions of Bodin's theory in Hancke, *Jean Bodin*, Breslau, 1900; Schmidt, *Allgemeine Staatslehre*, Leipzig, 1901; and Jellinek, *Allgemeine Staatslehre*, Berlin, 1905.

particular form of government. For him the essential basis of the State is supreme authority, which in French he calls "*souverainté*," and in Latin "*majestas.*" This he defines as "absolute and perpetual power," — "*puissance absolue et perpétuelle.*" It is from this source that laws proceed, and by it they are enforced. Without it there can be no State. In his further exposition he describes "sovereignty" as "absolute, indivisible, inalienable." Being absolute, it admits of no limitation; being indivisible, it cannot be shared or partitioned; being inalienable, it cannot be lost or taken away.

It is evident, that such a quality can only be attributed to that which is in itself a unit, which has a faculty of self-determination and a form of continuity. It is, therefore, most effectively represented by a person; and Bodin finds the natural bearer of it in a monarchical dynasty, which best fulfils all these conditions. Almost of necessity the attribute of sovereignty, as he conceives of it, implies the existence of a personal sovereign. His absence betokens some temporary accident or some imperfection in the organization of the State.

There were not wanting hostile critics of Bodin's doctrine even in his own day, but his conception of the State was so well adapted to sustain the existing order of his time that his theory of sovereignty became the foundation of nearly all subsequent political thought, and his book is still cited as an epoch-making work.

It is to Bodin, therefore, that we owe that conception of sovereignty which has proved to be the most serious theoretical obstacle to the assignment of a fixed and definite place to the State in the juristic order of ideas. If the State is absolute, has no superior, and is subject to no law, then it is impossible to organize the world in a juristic sense; and there must ever remain as many ungoverned, ungovernable, and purely arbitrary entities as there are Sovereign States, thus ensuring perpetual anarchy in the realm of international relations.

It is evident that Bodin's conception of the State places it in the category of Might and not in the category of Right. It possesses powers but not obligations, and leaves us in the presence of irresponsible and arbitrary autocracies.

THE PLACE OF THE STATE IN THE JURISTIC ORDER

Is it possible thus to conceive adequately of the State? The first problem of world organization is to fix the place of the State in the order of juristic thought, and this Bodin has entirely failed to do. The maxim, "*Princeps legibus solutus est*," cannot be accepted as a legal maxim; for, in making the ruler independent of all laws, it is only by arbitrary dogmatism that the idea of legal obligation can be furnished with a starting point. In some manner we must break into the circle of rights, or we are left in the circle of mere potencies; and it can never be proved that the power to compel obedience is a ground or reason for the obligation of obedience.

This was clearly perceived by Johann Althusius (1557–1638),[1] who, living in Holland at the time when a new State was actually forming from the fragments of the liberated Spanish Netherlands, was brought into closer contact with the problem. Perceiving that the State can be founded only on some principle of unity, and that it must exercise over its constituents some kind of supremacy, Althusius also took

---

[1] Gierke, *Johannes Althusius und die Entwickelung der naturrechtlichen Staatstheorien*, Breslau, 1902; Althusius, *Politica*, Herborn, 1603.

up the word "sovereignty"; but defined it as "a *right* indivisible, incommunicable, and imprescriptible, inherent in the whole body politic."

Thus conceived, sovereignty is the "right" to form and maintain a State possessed by a free group of human beings dwelling in a given territory. Reduced to its simplest terms, it is simply the right of a free community to provide for self-regulation and to maintain its own existence.

Such a right is axiomatic, and springs directly from a social need. Sovereignty, in this sense, is indeed the foundation and the substance of a State. But, thus conceived, it belongs not to the category of Might but to the category of Right. Being the expression of a moral necessity, it possesses a moral character. It is rooted and grounded in the rights inherent in personality. The State, thus conceived, demands obedience not merely because it has power to enforce its commands, but because it is the expression of the collective will for the realization of human rights.

It was this conception of the State that rendered it possible for Grotius (1583–1645) to carry the juristic idea into the wider field of international relationships, and to construct a science of universal jurisprudence. Starting with the Law of Nature inherent in the reason of man, with the aid of the principles of the Roman law, — well fitted in so many respects to meet the requirements of law universal, — he developed a system of jurisprudence for the government of nations. As reason is common to all men and all men are kindred, States have an essential community of nature, and belong to a higher form of society. In war, says Grotius, laws are silent; but not those laws which in the juristic order of thought should be observed even in the time of war; for law, whether or not it is respected, never abdicates the throne of

Reason. Its Majesty is alone supreme, and the only true sovereignty is the sovereignty of Law.

It was a new age, for human thought at least, that was ushered in by the great work of Grotius on "The Rights of War and Peace" (1625).[1] In him Machiavelli met his great adversary. Bodin had tried to vindicate the reasonableness of absolutism, for which Machiavelli had furnished the rules of action. Althusius had enunciated the true conception of the State, founded upon rights, embodying the security of rights, and subject to the rule of right. Grotius pointed the lesser and local sovereignties to that higher and universal sovereignty expressed in the essential unity of mankind and the supremacy of reason as the highest human attribute.

Since that day there has been in the world a struggle between two opposing conceptions of the State, and of the relations between States: the Machiavellian conception, based on arbitrary power, unlimited and irresponsible; and the Althusian conception, based on inherent rights, limited powers, and organized securities.

All the great contests which have marked the advance of civilization have been fought out on the battlefields of thought before they have been finally decided in the realm of action. This conflict of views is not yet ended, but the gains for the juristic idea have been considerable. Its victories are unequal in different parts of the world, and this is what renders a general world organization still an unsolved problem. For the final solution of it we may have long to wait. Civilization has always proceeded by refluent movements, and a steady and uninterrupted advance has seemed

---

[1] Grotius, *De Jure Belli ac Pacis*, Amsterdam, 1625.

too much for human energies; but no penetrable path of human progress has ever yet been pointed out to which, after straying from the way or reposing to renew its strength, humanity has not returned with new hope and fresh courage, resolved to push forward in its journey toward the light.

II

THE STATE AS A JURISTIC PERSON

As the embodiment of law, the State has a fixed place in the juristic order of thought. Through its power of compulsion it belongs to the category of Might, but its authority to command obedience is derived from the category of Right. If the latter had no existence, the State could make no appeal to our consciences, and present no rational ground for our obedience. Its claims upon us, having no moral basis, would depend entirely upon its use of force and our inability to resist it.

The Machiavellian theory of the State frankly admits this, and rests its whole case upon the supremacy of arbitrary power. Mankind, it affirms, is essentially corrupt and perverse; and, if left to itself, would accomplish its own self-destruction through its inherent predisposition to disorder and anarchy. The Prince appears upon the scene, quells the commotions of the mob, establishes public order, dictates law and sees that it is enforced. Whatever rights exist are created through this process. All governments are local, because it is impossible to prescribe universal order; but the Prince should be as absolute as he can be; and, in order to become so, he must in every way augment his power. The wider his area of territory, the greater the force he has at his command; and the more he can bind neighboring princes to his policies, the more sure is he that the State will persist and dominate over its enemies within and without his realm.

There being no basis for *inherent rights*, — which are mere personal illusions, having no existence in nature, — even the State can have no rights, except such as it can vindicate by force. It is, upon this theory, essentially *non-moral*.

THE ALTHUSIAN POSTULATE OF INHERENT RIGHTS

In contradiction to this view, Althusius, Grotius, and all the jurists who have followed them presuppose a natural moral order underlying all human relations, and obtaining recognition in the State, which is its institutional expression.

Like many other postulates of thought and action, that of a natural moral order is incapable of logical demonstration. If we say that such an order is revealed to us by the faculty of reason, it may be asked, What then is "reason"? If we reply, that reason is a power of insight by which we apprehend the existence of certain principles, it may be rightly objected, that, instead of proving our postulate, we are only stating it in another form. If, again, we seek the proof of a moral order in some kind of feeling that makes its first appearance in mankind, we seem to rely upon a mere deliverance of our own inner consciousness.

But the moralist and the jurist are in this regard not in worse plight than the mathematician, who gives law to all our natural sciences, and to whom all the less exact forms of knowledge appeal for certainty whenever possible; for the mathematician cannot prove his axioms, and if you do not accept them without proof, he simply tells you, that you cannot be a mathematician, and closes the door of the temple of exact knowledge in your face.

The wisdom of life, and even science itself, consists largely in a choice between alternatives. Theorists have debated over the question whether laws were first, and rights came into being as consequences of them; or whether rights were first, and laws were meant to give them security; but this problem has little practical importance, and is like the puzzle over the question whether the egg existed before the bird, or the bird before the egg. It is the fashion in some influential quarters to hold, with Machiavelli, that rights are the progeny of law; and to deny the existence of any natural rights whatever. It is not essential to a juristic conception of the State to refute this contention; for no one can doubt, whatever their origin, and whatever the real origin of the State may be, that rights — personal rights, and even moral rights — are the present and necessary foundation of society, as it exists to-day. The atmosphere of discussion is effectually cleared by simply asking the question, Can we live together a single day, or a single hour, without assuming, asserting, and recognizing the existence of both moral and jural rights, actually possessed by every person?

If we stop for a moment to consider the Machiavellian doctrine that the State is "non-moral," we at once perceive that it is not only a theory of the State but a theory of life. And it is a very inconsistent theory; for, if *all men* are "totally depraved," and possess no "inherent rights," there remains no standard for measuring their "depravity," or for assuming that they are "depraved." Nor is there any ground for asserting that disorder and crime are less commendable than order and obedience to law; which, at best, in a strictly non-moral system, are merely the results of physical compulsion.

But the truth is, we cannot even imagine the existence of a "non-moral" form of human society. If it were "non-moral," it would not be human; for there does not exist upon the earth a tribe of savages so low that there is in it no moral sense whatever. If there were, we should recoil from it as something worse than bestial; for it would be unnatural that a being endowed with intelligence fit to be classed as human should utterly ignore the existence of rights and duties.

We say "unnatural," because, whatever its origin, this perception has an objective, permanent, and absolute basis in nature. In the manifold transformations of the physical world, there is constancy in the sum of existing forces. This permanence in the midst of change is the only form of the absolute we know. All diversities are dependent upon it and derived from it. For every credit on the books of nature there is a corresponding debit, and when the books are balanced every entry is accounted for.

There is then in the nature of things an equilibrium of having and yielding, which may be regarded as the primary law of all relative being. When we ascend from inanimate forces to the biological realm, we perceive that living things form societies whose existence is dependent on mutuality, and both plant and animal instincts feel the difference between the way to life and the way to death. In the human world begins the consciousness of relation between possession and obligation, becoming always clearer as intelligence develops. Upon this level the correct balance between debits and credits is grasped in the concept of "justice," the rendering to each that which is his due; which is to the moral and jural world what equilibrium is to the physical world. As without equilibrium there could be no natural cosmos, so without justice there can be no human cosmos. In the one we speak of "equilibrium," in the other of "equity"; but it is the same Law of Nature that runs through all things, and in the midst of relative instability gives to the component forces of the world, through ceaseless readjustment, the stability of a universe.

Emerging into conscious personality, self-centred, self-determining, self-expressive, these relations give rise to the concepts of "right" and "wrong," of that which "ought" and that which "ought not" to be done; and thus is created the moral and the jural orders of thought. We build our lives and our hopes upon these fecund contingencies, these possibilities of unfulfilled but ever evolving ideals. Thence arise human institutions, of which the greatest is the State. It is not a mere artifice, it is not a casual association for personal or collective emolument, it is the fulfilment of nature's principle of balance and coördination in the relations of human life. To speak of it as "non-moral," is to ignore the struggles, the aspirations, and the sacrifices of all the great patriots, statesmen, and heroes of liberty who have made it what it is.

GROTIUS' IDEA OF LAW IMPOSED BY NATURE

Historically considered, the idea that moral distinctions are inherent in the constitution of man is one of the oldest of all juristic conceptions. The Stoic philosophy, which exercised so profound an influence upon Roman ideas of law, asserted the existence of a Law of Nature, — to be carefully distinguished from "natural laws" in the modern scientific sense, — which discloses in the consciousness of man a knowledge of rights and obligations. *Jus Naturae*, as the Romans called it, is the primary source of *Jus Gentium*, or law common to all nations; because nature has implanted in man universally the faculty of reason, which provides principles by which right and wrong may be distinguished. According to

Justinian, *Jus Naturae*, the Law of Nature, is inherent in the whole human race; *Jus Gentium*, the Law of Nations, is derived from it in the course of human experience; *Jus Civile*, or Civil Law, is the law of a particular community, preeminently that of Rome.

It was to these distinctions that Grotius recurred in his efforts to establish a universal jurisprudence. He reclassifies law, dividing it, first, into Natural and Voluntary. Voluntary Law is subdivided into divine, which is revealed moral law; and human, which includes Civil Law, and the Law of Nations, which he employs to mean the law governing the conduct of the society of States. In the course of his discussion he constantly contrasts the Law of Nature and the Law of Nations.[1]

This last distinction is important to remember, for upon it Grotius bases the principle of juristic progress, rendered necessary by the growth and development of civilized society. The Law of Nations is for him the sum of principles and practices actually in use; the Law of Nature consists of "the dictates of right reason," by which men are to be guided in perfecting their social relations, and should therefore be constantly applied for the improvement of the society of States. He thus places himself in a position to affirm without self-contradiction that there is in existence a body of rules voluntarily recognized as applicable to the conduct of States in their relations to one another; and at the same time that these accepted rules are capable of extension, revision, and improvement, in the light of experience and rational judgment.

It is not just to reproach Grotius with pedantry, because, in his efforts to establish a general consensus of opinion with

[1] Grotius, *De Jure Belli ac Pacis*, Prolegomena, XLIII.

regard to great principles, he abounds in citations that are often tedious, even superfluous, and sometimes wrested from their original purpose. "In order to give proofs on questions respecting Natural Law," he says, "I have made use of the testimonies of philosophers, historians, poets, and, finally, orators. Not that I regard these as judges from whose decision there is no appeal; for they are warped by their party, their argument, their cause, — but I quote them as witnesses whose conspiring testimony, proceeding from innumerable different times and places, must be referred to some *universal cause*, which, in the questions with which we are concerned, cannot be any other than a right deduction proceeding from the proofs of reason, or some other common consent."[1] In so far as these agreements point to the dictates of reason, they indicate the presence of the Law of Nature. In so far as they point to common consent, they reveal the existence of a voluntarily admitted Law of Nations.

The really influential part of the work of Grotius is not the opinions which he has collected or which he personally approves, many of which do not bear close examination. It is rather his indication of a source of law, ever fresh and inexhaustible, from which may be drawn clearer and better defined rules of action. "The dictates of right reason" were not exhausted by his authorities or by himself. So long as human experience lasts, widening with the years and with the centuries, that fountain will never cease to flow. In overstepping the narrow judgments and precepts of his time, — a time peculiarly characterized by cruelty, crudity, superstition, and bigotry, — Grotius entered upon the endless road of human progress, and set the thought of his race upon an ever ascending highway.

[1] Grotius, *De Jure Belli ac Pacis*, Prolegomena, XLI.

But what is most characteristic of Grotius is his faith in the moral element of Natural Law. His conception of the universe was vital, not mechanical. He was a prophet of the biologic age, when men were to cast aside the idea of fixity and finality in the order of nature, and to see in it the promise and potency of greater things. The idea of natural evolution probably never occurred to him, but he had the spirit of that great law. He saw that neither man nor society was a finished product. He perceived that both were to go on to greater heights of perfection and attainment. But his faith was not built upon a knowledge of the unity of force and the universality of natural laws, which science has since made evident to us. He did not know that the stars in their courses were fighting for his cause. What he did know was, that man and society were at war; at war with what was best in their own nature; at war with the idea of law, of justice, and of brotherhood. He died before the Thirty Years' War — that holocaust of violence, ambition, and revenge — was ended. The Peace of Westphalia of 1648, by which it was terminated, was a peace that would have gladdened his heart; for, imperfect and sordid as it was, it recognized what had never been acknowledged before, the society of independent States, and their obligations to maintain a peace based upon a general compact; the first peace inspired by the idea of law since the days of the *Pax Romana*.

PUFENDORF'S IDEA OF THE STATE AS A MORAL PERSON

In his great work on "The Rights of War and Peace," Grotius used the Law of Nature as a needed corrective of the Law of Nations, — that is, the customs of nations, — wherever these, as was frequently the case, were so savage or so unreasonable as to shock his moral sense. War, he held, though necessarily fraught with cruelties, might still be right; but, in order to be right, it must be just, and it must be prosecuted in accordance with just regulations. Assuming, as he did, that custom could create law, he nevertheless denied its positive force, if not in harmony with the Law of Nature.

A serious impediment to the erection of a system of international jurisprudence based on custom — the only positive foundation then known for law as universal, aside from the indefinite precepts of the Law of Nature — was the diversity and even the contradiction that existed among the usages of nations. The oldest rules that could be described as law international were the rules of maritime warfare, but unfortunately they were without uniformity. The ancient sea-laws of the Mediterranean permitted neutral property to pass free on enemy's ships, while enemy's property on board neutral ships was confiscated; and these rules were largely adopted in the Atlantic also, being at that time recognized by England, Portugal, and Holland; but France applied the rule, *robe d'ennemi confisque robe d'ami*, and the enemy's ship was confiscated with all its goods, including those of neutrals.

The first great apostle of the doctrines of Grotius was Pufendorf (1632-1694), who filled at Heidelberg the first university professorship of International Law ever established. In his work, "De Jure Naturae et Gentium" (1672), the prevailing customs of nations were almost entirely eliminated from consideration, as being too uncertain or unreasonable to be regarded as worthy of acceptance as law; and the Law of Nations was by him practically identified with the Law of Nature, from which in that work the controlling principles were almost exclusively derived.

The substantial identification of the Law of Nations with the Law of Nature by Pufendorf could naturally have no other practical effect than to leave an impression of doubt upon the reader as to the real existence of a body of international rules that could be called "law," in any other sense than moral law, or international ethics. The question of what a State *ought* to do in given circumstances, considered apart from the question of what States are *accustomed* to do, or by the rules agreed upon among them are *bound* to do, is plainly a question not of law in any jural sense, but merely one of morality.

The only manner, therefore, in which such a system of natural ethics could be construed as a system of International Law would be to show that States are in some way legally bound by the moral law, and that the sum and substance of the law properly governing the society of States is simply the code of morality applied to the peculiar relations in which States find themselves placed with regard to one another.

This is precisely what Pufendorf undertook to do. He defined the State as a *"moral person,"* who ought to act just as a good man ought to act.[1]

After the shock to our good sense and our consciences occasioned by a study of Machiavelli's conception of the State as essentially "non-moral," it is refreshing, and even comforting, to hear the State described as a "moral person," which seems at first thought to prepare the way for demonstrating the existence of rights and obligations by which the society of States may be rightly governed; but we are here compelled to ask

[1] According to Pufendorf's theory, the State is, in fact, to be identified with its ruler. His conception of the "persona moralis" is well explained by Gierke, *Johannes Althusius*, pp. 88, 89; who also gives an account of the historical development of the idea of the personality of the State, pp. 189, 210.

ourselves, if, in reality, States are so similar to individuals that both can be properly governed by the same laws.

THE STATE CONSIDERED AS A PERSON

First of all, arises the question if the State can, in any defensible sense, be considered as a "person." In reflecting upon this assumption, we perceive at once that an association of human beings jurally related under accepted laws, and occupying a certain extent of territory, is at least quite different from a natural person. When, however, we consider that a State is essentially a unit among other units of like kind, forming a society and governed by law, of which it is the embodiment; that it is a union of forces having a definite object, and organized for the accomplishment of that object; that it is endowed with a public consciousness of itself, of its purpose, and of its relations; that it is capable of determining its actions by the power of choice inherent in its collective will; in short, that it is not only an organized unit, but possesses intelligence and voluntary power of action, through its constituted organs of expression, it does not seem altogether fantastic to think of it as belonging to the class of beings known as "persons," rather than to the class of beings known as "things." When, in addition, we reflect upon the fact, that the State can both receive and bestow benefits and injuries, intelligently offered or withheld, it is evident also that it is endowed with rights and obligations as clearly and as really as any human individual. The fact of personality in man may defy our power of analysis and lead us into the deepest mystery of philosophy, but it does not embarrass our power of description; and, if we follow the lines of analogy, we are compelled to conclude that, in the qualities just enumerated, a

State is more like a person than any other form of existence to which it may be compared.

We are not surprised, therefore, to learn that practically all modern jurists are in agreement with Pufendorf in assigning the attribute of personality to the State. It may be granted, that it is only by analogy that the word "person" may be thus applied; but it must also be conceded, that it is far more appropriate to the State than the designation "Leviathan," used by Thomas Hobbes (1588–1679), or that of "mechanism," which leaves out of account the most essential and distinctive characteristics of the State, namely, self-consciousness, intelligence, and the power of self-determination. If it be objected that these cannot be localized in the State, except as functions of its constituent members and its representative organs of legislative, judicial, and executive decision and action, it may be asked, in reply, "What do we know of the functions of personality in the human individual except in connection with the organic complex by which they are differentiated, unified, and expressed?"

We may, therefore, with sufficient scientific warrant, ascribe the attributes of personality to the State, and thereby recognize the fact, that it has relations to the Law of Nature similar to those which characterize the human individual; or, as Pufendorf expresses it, "the natural man." We may, without importing fallacy into our exposition, go so far as to say, that the State for the same reasons as the "natural man," has rights and duties. Nor can we escape the conclusion, that because it has not always existed in the form it now possesses, or in the most primitive conditions of human society in any form whatever, that it is, in reality, less the product of nature than man himself. The course of natural development is a continuous one, — not perhaps in an evenly ascending scale of unbroken advancement, for there are long periods of relative rest in the labors of nature, — but continuous in the sense that the nexus between cause and effect is known to us in the guise of an evolution from lower to higher forms of existence, over the whole of which nature presides as an ever present determining agent. The philosopher as well as the infant, the State as well as the family, are linked with the past and with the whole system of natural forces and their inherent laws by the same chain of rational necessity. The State is not an arbitrary artifice. It is not an artifice at all. It is the jural expression of Man the Species, as distinguished from man the individual. It could not come before its natural time, but in its own place in the order of development it could not fail to come.

THE RELATION OF THE STATE TO MORAL LAW

If these propositions express the truth, we cannot escape the conclusion of Pufendorf, that the State is, in some sense, not only a "person" but a "moral person." We shall, no doubt, be compelled to set limits to this conception, if we apply it in any other than a purely ideal sense; for there is too much truth in Machiavelli's notion of the State as "non-moral" in the forms in which it has existed and still exists. But before we proceed to trace some of the necessary limitations, let us consider for a moment the relation of the State to the moral law.

The moral law, as we have previously mentioned, vindicates itself in the consequences that follow upon the violation of it. There is no force in nature, and there is no force in human society, that can compel obedience to it; for the reason that it is a law that dictates directions for the inner life, for the

THE STATE AS A JURISTIC PERSON 39

dispositions, intentions, and desires, as well as for the forms of outward conduct. It is open at every point to disobedience and it is necessary that it should be; because it is a law of life, whose necessary alternative is death. It applies to nations, and to States as the embodiments of law, as well as to individual human beings. It is even easier to take note of the penalties consequent upon the violation of moral law in the case of nations than in the case of individual men. "Without doubt," says a high authority, "States are able to do as they please, but it is not in their power to avoid the effects which their acts produce; and, while these effects most frequently escape the attention or the consciousness of contemporaries, they are none the less certain. If a State follows a violent and vexatious policy in regard to its neighbors, it may compel them to endure it as long as it remains the stronger, but it provokes and excites animosities which eventually break forth against it. If a State concludes a treaty of commerce and feels itself strong enough to impose its tariffs upon a weaker State, it can do so; but, if its calculations are erroneous, it ruins itself. If a State dictates to a vanquished adversary an abusive treaty, it is not the establishment of peace, but the preparation of war. . . . It may be that, in the space of a human life, the time may not be sufficient for these consequences to manifest themselves, but they are revealed later on; and they reveal themselves infallibly. Statesmen may sometimes enjoy impunity, because they die; nations cannot escape the penalty for ever, because they live long enough to undergo the consequence of their acts." [1]

"The fathers have eaten sour grapes, and their children's teeth are set on edge." Moral law has its sanction in the

[1] Funck-Brentano and Sorel, *Précis du Droit des Gens*, Paris, 1877, Introduction and p. 7.

sequences which Nature has ordained, and although the seed may be long in maturing, the harvest comes at last, whether it be of good or of evil. A policy of spoliation vitiates the national character of the people who practice it, and when the State is no longer able to rob its neighbors the strong will oppress and despoil the weak at home, because extortion has become the habitual practice. An indemnity unjustly wrung from a conquered nation will be spent many times over in maintaining the force to prevent the endeavors of the vanquished to win back what they have lost. The years may veil the unobserved readjustment of the balance, but the future will always be counted upon to redress the wrongs of the past.

Nothing then is more certain than that States are subject to the penalties of violated moral law; and yet it is obvious, that it is not in its full sense applicable to States; and that it is not the only, nor even the principal, form of law by which States are governed in their relations to one another.

It cannot be maintained that morality as applied to the life and conduct of individuals is also applicable to States, in the sense that a State can and should always act exactly as a good man would act. The reason for this is found in the essential difference between a State and an individual; a man being constituted for a highly diversified general experience, while a State exists for specific purposes.

The moral law, taken in its entirety, includes the whole realm of personal feelings, specifically the dispositions of the heart. Charity, benevolence, pity, preeminently the love of God and the love of our neighbor, are for the human individual essential parts of morality; but it would be difficult to imagine these as required of the State, or even as possible to it.

The State is a "moral person" in the sense of possessing rights and obligations, and being subject to moral law; but only in so far as these comport with its nature. When closely examined, it is evident that it is not endowed with a capacity for sentiment or emotion. It may register in its experience the consequences of its acts, as it must do under the law of causation, from which it is not exempt; but it cannot feel penitence for its sins, it cannot ask for grace, it cannot hope for mercy.

The formula of morality for the State is found in the principles of equity and justice. The State *is* equity and justice, duly organized and become conscious of themselves. It is in reality nothing else than the jural side of man's nature in its community organization. A, and B, and X, Y, and Z live in a community. If none of these constituents had a sense of their reciprocal jural relations, and these relations were in no way organized, evidently there would be no State. But now all these individuals become conscious of their jural relations; that is, of rights and obligations to be secured and enforced by law, and they proceed to make laws, or to accept laws from one another. The moment that is done the State exists as the embodiment of law, and their community thus organized, conscious of its unity, itself thereby charged with rights and duties towards its kind in other places, capable of self-direction and self-determination through its chosen organs, becomes a juristic person, as the sentient cell of a living organism, united in one body, provided with organs, and thus incorporating a conscious power of action, comes into being as a natural person. In neither case is the process of becoming a purely artificial one. In both instances, it was prepared for, and partially accomplished, at lower and unconscious stages of existence; and it has been completed through the operation of an inherent law of natural development at the moment when the necessary preconditions were combined.

THE INADEQUACY OF MORAL LAW FOR THE STATE

It is conceivable that a community of living beings, possessing moral instincts and following their admonitions, could live together without any other than moral law as revealed to the individual consciousness. If the conditions of life in such a community were uniform, only a few simple customs would be necessary; and if all were disposed to follow them, their lives might be harmonious, peaceable, and happy. It is evident, however, that, as the relations of the community became more complicated, its conditions more diverse, and the disposition to follow the few simple customs less controlling, attention would have to be given to the definition of rights and duties; explicit rules would have to be laid down, either by a superior or by common agreement, and these would have to be enforced. It is apparent also, that, in the relations of coexistent distinct communities, the same necessities would follow upon the increased complexity of their modes of existence, their encroachment upon one another, and their disposition to lay claim to the same lands or the same objects of value. If these communities became organized as States, and should become conscious of themselves as such, it would be necessary to lay down rules for their common observance. Before there was any voluntary attempt to formulate such rules, customs would have grown up, some of them sufficiently tolerable to endure and be perpetuated, others too unreasonable or intolerable to be approved; and these last would require to be changed, in order to bring them into conformity with the well-being of the society of States.

This is precisely what has happened in the course of human history, and it has been found that moral laws, by themselves, are not sufficient for the government either of any single community, or of States in their relations to one another. It has, therefore, been necessary to formulate particular rules which can be enforced; that is, jural laws, as distinguished from the precepts of morality binding only on the conscience.

According to the theory of international right propounded by Pufendorf, this was impossible; because States, being independent and sovereign, and having no common superior to impose and enforce such laws upon them, — which moreover he considered to be superfluous, — any kind of law other than moral law could not, he thought, be applied to States. All, therefore, were to be left to the dictates of their consciences; but, in the interest of peace, justice, and the general welfare, these dictates should be clearly formulated, recognized, and obeyed.

Upon this theory, International Law consists in counsels of perfection; binding, indeed, on States as "moral persons," but only morally binding. This is merely to commend to mankind the reverent endeavor to realize its own highest ideals in the relation of States as being a paramount duty; but without placing law upon any positive basis, or providing any means whatever for its enforcement. It is a confession, that the State, although itself the embodiment of law, and a "moral person," is of such a peculiar nature that it cannot be brought into any enforced juristic system. In effect, while far superior to Machiavelli's doctrine, that the State is essentially non moral, this theory has practically, for the enterprise of world organization, the same result; for it makes enforceable law end with the local State, and offers no provision for universal order, except the good intentions of human governments, which may be sincere, or may be merely illusory.

THE ALLEGED EXEMPTION OF THE STATE FROM MORALITY

In the swing of the pendulum of thought between the extreme positions, that the State is essentially "non-moral," and that it is a "moral person" charged with the full obligations of morality, there has appeared the doctrine that the State, although moral in its nature and purposes, may be exempted from a complete compliance with moral law, even in those respects where, under ordinary circumstances, it ought to be obeyed.

This doctrine has been very eloquently set forth by Gustav Ruemelin (1815–1889), in an address on "Politics and the Moral Law," delivered by him in 1874, as Rector of the University of Göttingen.

"Our natural impulses," he says, "as manifested in prevailing current opinions, would, with emphasis, unhesitatingly affirm that politics must be subject to the moral law. Yet we must admit, be the contradiction only real or only apparent, that there are certain actions permitted by the code of political ethics, but prohibited by the moral law. We praise those who have freed their people from bondage, rescued them from dismemberment, aroused them from impotent lethargy, and raised them to a higher plane of prosperity, power, and liberty. And yet we do not shut our eyes to the fact that these ends may have been accomplished by means utterly inadmissible under other conditions, — by intrigue and force, by blood and iron. On the other hand, we reproach a prince who, though gifted with an acute intellect, noble ambition, and a delicate moral sense, fails to appreciate, and leaves unfulfilled, the tasks set before him by his people and his age." [1]

As an illustration of what he means, Ruemelin cites the different degrees of esteem in which Frederick the Great is held, on the one hand as a writer, and on the other as a statesman. In his young manhood the king combated the teachings of Machiavelli with the most ardent zeal, and maintained that there could be no other standard but the moral law. "To be sure," says Ruemelin, "his book was written while he was still crown prince, and the politics of the king, although not in line with the principles taught by Machiavelli, followed more obscure and more devious paths than were dreamed of by the youthful author of the Castle of Rheinsberg. And yet it is undeniable, that posterity, as well as public opinion during Frederick's lifetime, have evinced less admiration for his books than for his deeds."

THE NECESSARY INTERPRETATION OF MORAL LAW

There are various attitudes likely to be assumed toward walking in "obscure and devious paths" for the sake of the State, by those who have profited by it, by those who have suffered from it, and by those who set themselves up as critics, or casuists, regarding the moral conduct of public men. At best, this is not a subject upon which agreement results from argument; for apologists and accusers alike usually start with opposite and invincible prejudices, and even the impartial judge cannot always fathom the motives by which action has been inspired.

---

[1] Ruemelin, *Reden und Aufsätze*, Tuebingen, 1874 and 1894, I, p. 144, translated by Rudolf Tombo, Jr., under the title, *Politics and the Moral Law*, New York, 1901.

It is, however, clear, that an unjust act done in the interest of the State does not cease to be unjust, because it is not performed for personal advantage; and it is difficult to see why the State, which stands for justice, should need that it be performed.

But a judgment regarding moral delinquency, whether in the case of a private person or a public power, in order to be sound, must take into consideration all the circumstances that attend the case. The same rules of conduct do not hold regarding what is due to a friend and to a robber, to an innocent visitor and to a midnight assassin. No deed can be justly condemned or applauded, unless it is taken in connection with its antecedents and its provocation. We cannot condemn President Lincoln, to take an example from our own history, as a robber because he emancipated the slaves of those who were in rebellion, although in so doing he deprived them of their most valuable property. The justification of his act is not merely that slavery itself is wrong, for it would have been justifiable even if slavery were right; because behind the act of emancipation was the higher mandate to hasten and confirm in permanence the national peace, which demanded that the cause of conflict be removed, and removed at once for ever. In the crises of nations, even more emphatically than in the lives of men, there are moments when existence hangs upon decision; and decision is often a choice between alternatives, either of which may involve some elements of wrong. In such instances it is not a violation of justice, even though our decision may occasion immense suffering, if the intention and effect of our action are in accordance with the higher mandate of the moral law that requires us to promote the greater good and suppress the greater evil. True morality, public or private, does not consist in obedience to the letter, which is dead; but to the spirit, which maketh alive.

It does not appear then that in choosing the less of two alternative evils, or in obeying the more mandatory of two incompatible commands, there is any violation of moral law; but there is ever present in such circumstances the necessity of correct interpretation. A government, or a public officer, acting as the representative of the State, is indeed more heavily burdened with responsibility than any private person can be. This cannot be better stated than by Ruemelin himself, who says: "The statesman is not divisible into two beings, of which one, the layman, would possess a conscience, the other, the politician, none. It is easy to prove, if anything, the very opposite. He who acts for others is placed under stricter obligations than he who acts for himself. It is no reproach to the individual if he neglects his own advantage. As guardian or trustee of another's property, the same neglect would render him liable to punishment. Upon the decisions of the leader of a State depends the welfare of millions; and, as their mandate is the highest, so is his moral responsibility the greatest."

THE RELATION OF A STATESMAN TO THE MORALITY OF PUBLIC POLICIES

"This fact," continues Ruemelin, "renders the politician alone subservient to the moral law as an individual; *the same is by no means true of his policy*. The very highest sense of moral obligation is enjoined upon the statesman, but the content of his duties is not thereby prescribed."

It is difficult to believe, that such contradictory statements can exist peaceably together in the same mind. There is, no doubt, much required by the moral law that does not apply to the State, because of its particular nature; but how can a man be governed by moral law as an individual and not be governed by it in his policies, if it be true, as we are assured, that he "cannot be divisible into two beings," one with a conscience, and another without one? Who, then, dictates his policies? What master has the right to impose upon him policies in which the moral law is not respected? Ruemelin answers, "The self-interest of the State."

It is admitted that justice is the element in which the State moves; that the sense of right is the ultimate source of its existence; and that the neglect of justice is the undermining of its foundation. "Nevertheless," we are told, "the relation of the State to justice differs essentially from that of the individual. . . . *The interests of a foreign State can be regarded only in so far as they do not conflict with our own.*"

It is true, that self-interest is the working basis of statesmanship, just as it is of private business, and the greater part of human activities; but is there in the nature of the State anything which makes self-interest the sole standard of public policy, and thereby dispenses statesmen from conformity to moral principles in their public acts?

In another academic address, delivered by Lord Lytton (1831-1891) before the University of Glasgow, in 1888, it was contended that the difference between the State and a private individual is of such a kind that the same rules of action could almost never apply.[1] As an illustration of this difference, the noble lord — a noted diplomatist who had served as Viceroy of India, and whose authority as a statesman was esteemed to be preeminent — stated, that an individual might regard it as a duty to sacrifice his life for the

[1] Printed in the London *Times*, for Nov. 10, 1888.

good of others, but no one could conceive it possible in any circumstances that it could ever be the duty of a nation to extinguish its existence for the benefit of another nation, or even for humanity at large. And, in order to emphasize the wide difference between a private person and a nation, it was asserted, "Individual Scotchmen may get drunk, but Scotland cannot!"

Without pausing to inquire what would be the condition of Scotland, if all Scotchmen should get drunk at the same time, we may pass to Lord Lytton's serious argument, that "a nation is not only entitled, but bound, to act with greater seeming selfishness than would be permitted to any single individual in like relations;" because nations are "aggregations of citizens, holding *each other's* interests in mutual trust." "The moral significance of what is called national selfishness," he says, "is thereby wholly changed, for it *ceases to be selfishness*, in any proper sense of the word, and *becomes patriotism*."

The substance of this argument is, that when the army and navy are set in motion to enforce the unjust claims, or as yet unrealized ambitions, of A and B and C, it is not "selfishness," but "patriotism," on the part of X and Y and Z, to applaud the action, and pay the bills!

PUBLIC AND PRIVATE MORALITY

It is quite impossible, by any form of sophistry, however ingenious, to make it appear that public men are not responsible for public policies; or that a whole nation possesses any characteristic which exempts it from common honesty and just dealing.

When Lord Lytton quotes a lord chancellor as saying, "A corporation has no body to be kicked, and no soul to be damned;" and adds, "The same is true of nations;" he is engaged in perpetuating an error which has destroyed empires and overthrown kingdoms. There is no body politic incapable of receiving deep and lasting wounds, and the spirit of cupidity in national policies has in most instances worked out a terrible eventual retribution. And yet, it is upon such reasoning, or rather such dogmatism, as that which denies to a nation both soul and body, that this brilliant rhetorician bases his conclusion, that "public and private morality differ so widely that hardly a single proposition applicable to the one can be properly applied to the other. . . . Only one obligation, namely, justice, has a place in public morals; and the sort of justice which finds its place in public morals is totally different from the justice which relates to private individuals. . . . It consists mainly in *moderation and kindly pretence!*"

To this attenuated conception of public morality, Lord Lytton adds the opinion, — not, however, substantiated by any reasoning, — that, while "lying, indifference to human suffering, rapacity, and cruelty do not lose their essential character because they are incidental to public actions, . . . we are not to judge statesmen as we should judge private persons."

In this elaborate restatement of Machiavellian theory, not one substantial reason has been advanced why a public officer should practice falsehood or inhumanity for the benefit of the State; or why the real interest of the State should require that political policies be supported by any of the crimes or vices for which extenuation is demanded.

To those who recall the circumstances in which Lord Lytton spoke, it is quite unnecessary to explain, that, although this last notable defence of Machiavellianism was made in the form of an academic address, it was by no means a calm and disinterested expression of academic judgment.

As an English historian has said, "the world had seen the strange sight of a brilliant and powerful ruler, who took precedence of ancient dynasties in India, retiring into private life at the bidding of votes silently cast in ballot-boxes, far away in islands of the north."[1] And, as another English historian has said, "The general election of 1880 was no mere swing of the pendulum. It was an emphatic condemnation, . . . and a judgment for the sober, righteous politics which are neither more nor less than morality enlarged."[2]

There has been, since that time, so far as our knowledge extends, no open championship of the doctrine, that men acting in a public capacity are exempt from the ordinary rules of private morality. On the contrary, it appears to be a growing conviction, that public policies should be in harmony with moral law. But even this is not sufficient. It is believed that the State, as a juristic person, is not free to choose what principles it will follow; but is bound by its very nature to act in obedience to positive laws, by which its rights and duties are explicitly defined. The means of enforcing those laws may still be inadequate or defective; and hence, in existing circumstances, the State must be strong enough to defend its rights, if they are invaded. But the more it is considered, the more widely it is realized that the ultimate source of a nation's strength is in the conscience of its people. It is ever becoming more clearly apparent, that good citizens endeavoring to live honest lives in accordance with just laws cannot consistently be urged to lend their force to any form of spoliation at the expense of other honest men belonging to other nations. No matter by what veil of sophistry it may be attempted to conceal the truth, true patriotism is not subservi-

[1] Rose, *The Development of European Nations*, London, 1905, p. 406.
[2] Paul, *A History of Modern England*, London, 1906, p. 137.

ency to the spirit of national greed, compounded of the selfishness or unjust demands of others, and claiming the right to wear the garb of altruism, on the ground that we do not profit by it! On the contrary, true patriotism cannot participate in the public sanction of that which would be dishonorable in ourselves. It is in its essential nature loyalty to the principles of justice and equity, on which the whole authority of the State reposes; and finds its highest satisfaction in rendering those principles everywhere triumphant over the unjust pretensions of arrogant and self-seeking men, and the fatal domination of oppressive policies.

III

THE STATE AS A PROMOTER OF GENERAL WELFARE

In characterizing the Modern State as an embodiment of law, and in pointing out its consequent place in the juristic order of thought, it is by no means intended to deny or obscure the fact, that it has important functions to perform which lie outside the field of jurisprudence. The territorial character of the Modern State imposes upon it many duties, and creates for it many rights and interests which demand the attention of those who are charged with the conduct of its affairs. Its course of activity cannot, therefore, be marked out for it in advance, and its freedom of choice is strictly necessary to the fulfilment of its destiny; for it is charged with the high responsibility of promoting the general welfare of its constituents.

It is, however, of importance to a correct knowledge of its proper place in a general system, to determine, if possible, how far, if at all, its juristic character is affected by the trust thus committed to its care.

THE DUTY OF THE STATE TO ITS CONSTITUENTS

There are many ways in which the State may contribute to the general welfare of the people who compose its population. It may undertake to construct and administer public utilities, too vast or too complicated for private or corporate enterprise. It may assume the support and direction of education, the management of the means of communication and transportation, the exploitation of natural resources, the advancement of science, the cultivation of art, and even the promotion of morality and religion. But none of these constitutes its distinctive and essential function; and, if any of them are entrusted to its oversight, it is because it is believed that in this way the greatest benefit may be obtained for the social organism. Not one of these functions, however, can be said to come within the sphere of the necessary duties of the State, unless it has already assumed responsibility for them; and being of a nature that might properly be entrusted to a private corporation, they cannot affect the nature of the State in its general character.

On the other hand, the protection of rights is the primary purpose for which the State exists; and this protection constitutes its preeminent obligation. Its juristic character, and this alone, confers upon it supreme authority over its constituents, and places its right to exist and to command above all discussion. Its fitness for the performance of other tasks may be open to debate, and may vary in particular circumstances; but so long as it continues faithful to its essential nature, it remains unassailable.

All history confirms this position; for there has rarely been a successful revolt against a government that faithfully and intelligently maintained the true character of the State as the just protector of human rights. Revolutions have in almost all cases been the protest of men, either wronged or oppressed, against some form of injustice or bad administration. The State has never proved a failure except when turned aside from its normal purpose and made to serve ends for which it was not constituted.

From this it appears that the real strength as well as the

intrinsic dignity of a government lies in the highest fulfilment of juristic ideals. Whatever its material support may be, it can in this way, and in this way only, associate with itself the moral forces of the nation.

Although the State belongs distinctively to the juristic order so far as its essential nature is concerned, it is for that very reason required to take an active part in the realm of material action. In order to compel obedience to law, it is often necessary to employ force, and sometimes armed force. As the embodiment of right, — and not at all because it is superior to the rules of ordinary action, — it may compel obedience to its laws, and protect its own existence against every form of attack. Being by its very nature the consecration of force to the realization of justice, it is in its own territories supreme over every form or combination of power. It can tolerate no *imperium in imperio*, whether it be in the form of great or aggregated wealth, organized societies, or associated interests; and it may rightly oppose and destroy every form of active or passive defiance of its authority.

It has been said, that, being thus autonomous, the State exists for itself. This is a misconception. It exists to serve the purposes for which it was constituted, that is, the realization and protection of the rights of its constituents. It is not then an end in itself, and has no right which is not based upon the rights it was created to secure.

THE STATE AND ITS GOVERNMENT

And here we are brought face to face with the distinction between the State and a government, or a form of government. A government must consist of persons acting in the name of the State, but they can act only in a representative manner; they do not constitute the State. Their conduct must be legal, or they do not even represent the State. Nor is any particular form of government essential to its purpose. A government may be in form a monarchy, an oligarchy, or a democracy, so long as it really stands for law and order, and is capable of maintaining them. The right to create the State includes the right to choose the form it shall assume; and the excellence of this form, in any given instance, is to be judged entirely by its adaptation to the genius of the people, their traditions, capacities, and preferences.

The essential function of the State being to act as the guardian of rights, its chief task consists in securing them to every individual. But it is not so easy, as it may at first sight appear, to determine what the rights of the individual are. The question of rights is fundamentally one of personality, for every person possesses rights; but it is also closely correlated to the whole course of social evolution, for new rights are generated at every point of the process of development. The rights of the child, of the adult, of the parent, of marriage, of citizenship, and many others unfold with the development of the individual and his enlarged relations to society. The State follows him into these new relations, or rather anticipates his entrance into them, and prepares his protection beforehand.

In addition to his rights, there is another set of objects dear to the individual which the State is often able to promote and protect, namely, his "interests." There is a strong motive for a government to look after the "interests" of its constituents, even when they do not have the form of rights; for this aids in rendering the government acceptable to those whose wishes it favors or helps to realize. It is always esteemed a great convenience to be able to use the power of the State for the furtherance of private ends, either in the form of exemptions, monopolies, or special kinds of privilege; and every government is likely to be tempted to make friends by affording this convenience to its most powerful supporters; but here lies a path of danger.

No one could profess that a group of persons occupying a given territory could set up an association for purposes of plunder, or even for mutual gain, and claim for it recognition as a State. It is equally clear, that a group of persons having temporary possession of a government may not employ it for predatory purposes, covering their enterprise with the aegis of the State, even when the profits are equally and fairly shared by the whole population.

THE DEFENCE OF NATIONAL INTERESTS

But there are certain "national interests" which seem at first sight to permit the exercise of the full power of the State in their behalf. These are the general interests of industry, trade, commerce, and the exploitation of partly or wholly uncivilized countries, which the State, and the State only, can promote and protect; interests which have a public character, because they affect the prosperity of the country as a whole, and especially in its business competition with other countries. What is to be said of these?

It would be a dangerous proposition to affirm that a State may everywhere, without qualification, pursue its material interests according to the full measure of its physical strength; and especially that it may use its army and navy for this purpose. It is well known, that governments are not only tempted to do this, but often yield to the temptation, and do actually so employ them; and it would be easy to cite examples, even of an extremely odious character. Take, as notorious instances, the policy of forcing China to admit opium against the wishes of the public authorities; and the use of warships to collect arbitrarily imposed indemnities for injuries never really committed, or entirely out of proportion to the wrongs actually done, without even the pretence of a judicial examination.

It is this purely arbitrary use of force in the support of real or alleged "interests" which renders the preponderating power of some nations over others so great a menace, and tends to stimulate even the smaller or weaker ones to join in the race for greater armaments.

It is evident, that the strenuous pursuit of so-called "interests" not having the definite form of rights is likely at any moment to bring great powers into collision, as well as to perpetrate shameful injustice upon the small and weak. It is the source of endless anxiety, and even of a chronic state of alarm. It has the support of all adventurers, who find their profit in thus perverting the powers of the State; but it is in opposition to the will and purpose of the far greater number of honorable and faithful citizens of every country, who by their industry and legitimate enterprise supply the resources which give power to the State.

It is, of course, not intended to suggest, that a government should be indifferent to its own real interests, or those of its constituents. On the contrary, it should maintain and protect them in every honorable way. It should see that the State it represents is denied no right accorded to others in foreign lands, and that its citizens everywhere receive just treatment. For these objects the whole force of the State, if necessary, should be exercised; for this is its normal function and obligation.

What needs to be emphatically and repeatedly pointed out is, that the one supreme interest of every State is, that it should firmly and fearlessly maintain its juristic character. This is its best protection from commotion and revolt within and from aggression from without. As the embodiment of law, it should stand bravely for the extension of legal procedure and the suppression of the rule of force, curbing predatory elements within its territories and the exercise of their influence abroad. Unjust exactions not only weaken its prestige but denature its very being, for they render inconsequent those principles of justice which the State is instituted to make effective.

THE DEVELOPMENT OF A NATIONAL CONSCIENCE

It is a gratification to see many signs of a general growth of public opinion in this respect. As in the development of an individual, so also in the progress of a political community, it is to be expected, that a lively appreciation of rights and interests will be experienced before the solemn consciousness of duties. A well-organized State is the result of the determination to protect the rights of persons and property by just laws. When this has been accomplished within the State, it is easy for a community to fix its attention upon the solidarity of its own interests, as against the rest of the world, and to overlook the rights of other communities. This is merely a sign of imperfect development; which, however, need not be permanent. But at this stage of growth, nations usually pass through a period when they think of themselves as entirely distinct entities, without bonds of common interest and obligation uniting them with other nations; just as young children often centre their thoughts entirely upon their own immediate desires, until their moral sense is awakened. Savage tribes continue, under arrested development, permanently to exist upon this lower level, living in a state of perpetual isolation and instinctive hostility to one another; but in the process of civilization communities gradually extend their sense of social solidarity beyond their borders, until it embraces others of like kind.

It seemed a new thought, when, in the first quarter of the seventeenth century, Grotius wrote: "If no community can subsist without observing some standard of right, as Aristotle proves by the example of brigands — who are obliged to recognize some principle of equity among themselves — with greater reason the human race, or a number of peoples, cannot dispense with it." [1]

We of course perceive, when we stop to think of it, that there is the same reason for establishing perfect justice between different nations as between different men of the same nation; but tribes of savages and bands of brigands do not take this view. Their idea is, not to create institutions of justice, but to obtain plunder. For this purpose, they find coöperation and organization necessary; but the distribution of booty incidentally reveals the existence of rights, which then demand satisfaction. Even among savages and brigands, the necessity of taking rights into account becomes evident; but here the community has not yet made them the basis, and continues to treat them only as the accident, of its social existence.

In the case of civilized States, it is quite otherwise. These are not associations formed for plunder, or even for profit. The Modern State is the public institution of rights, and does not belong to the predatory or mercenary order. It has

[1] Grotius, *De Jure Belli ac Pacis*, Prolegomena, XXIV.

passed from the level of barbarism to the level of civilization, and cannot escape the sense of being culpable when it pursues the methods of a barbarian horde; even though, by means of superior strength, it may act with impunity.

GOVERNMENT AS THE CURATOR OF THE STATE

When, therefore, a government even momentarily drops from the level of juristic action, and drags the forces of the State down to the level of a predatory community, it denatures the institution it professes to represent; for, in seeking an end which is not determined by a right, it is no longer acting as a State should act.

Yet it must not be forgotten, that, as an instrument of the general welfare, the State is expected to protect and promote "interests" as well as "rights," when these are of a collective nature; that is, the interests of the body politic as a whole. It is not merely a juristic, it is also an economic entity. It owns property, collects revenue, incurs financial obligations, and in a general sense superintends and organizes the material prosperity of its constituents. There are interests with which the State is essentially concerned. It is specifically charged with responsibility for the manner in which the industrial and commercial welfare of the people is affected by the conduct of other States, particularly as respects the extension or restriction of foreign markets; the opportunity of its nationals to share in enterprises in which they desire to participate in the less developed countries; and the fate of territories coveted for this purpose by other powers, which desire to reserve them for their own exclusive benefit.

By what process then is it possible to determine whether an "interest" may be pursued as a "right;" and may, therefore, be protected by all the force at the disposal of the State?

It must be admitted, that this determination is not always easy. There are many national interests which at first seem real and important to us, but do not partake of the nature of rights. We wish, for example, to secure a market for our goods in a foreign country, and it is clearly our national interest to do so; but we cannot claim to have a positive right to that market. The people of a foreign nation may buy of whom they please, or not at all; and we have no right either to compel them to buy of us, or to condemn them because they do not buy what they do not want. Yet, if they do buy of others and discriminate against us, we feel that they have withheld from us what is our due. An interest — by which we mean in this connection merely an advantage *in posse*, — may then easily assume the form of a right, when it falls into the category of equal opportunity. We seem quite justified in claiming the abstract right to an equal chance.

But such a right, admitting its existence, would have to be further examined before it could be given a concrete form, and could hardly be defended by force of arms. If we looked for the reason of this discrimination, we might perhaps find it in our own previous conduct; or in some special reciprocity arrangement; or, finally, in a determination to be unfriendly. We should then have to judge what our conduct should be in return.

THE FUNCTION OF DIPLOMACY

And here it becomes plain, before we go farther into this question, that, apart from the jural relations that ought to exist between nations, there are relations of a more general character which may be described as social relations. States are independent entities which, in their powers of mutual benefit and injury, and their attitudes of friendliness and hostility, are much like natural persons. They need, therefore, to recognize and maintain, as it were, social relations outside of their jural relations. These must be mediated through living persons, for good neighborhood can never be reduced to mere mechanism. There is required a constant interchange of courtesies, of friendly communication, of reassurance, and of explanation. This is the function of diplomacy; a function sometimes regarded as superfluous, but in reality immensely important, and even absolutely necessary to continued good understanding and amicable relations. If neighbors never met, except in the courts and in disputes over their respective rights and wrongs, there would be small prospect of a peaceful state of society.

It is precisely in the sphere of "interests" that are not yet perfect rights, that the diplomatist finds his chief field of usefulness. He represents "interests" far more than established rights. He builds interests into rights. He frames and interprets treaties, which furnish a positive foundation for rights. He recalls their existence, sees that they are applied, and where they fall short seeks to extend them, or at least to see that the nations continue to be on speaking terms. No slight or useless task is that, to smooth the way to right understandings, and in his person to furnish a channel through which reason, and kindliness, and mutual comprehension may have free passage.

Through that continuous intermediation, which can never judiciously boast of its own successes, and thrives best when least ostentatious, "interests" not only assume the form of "rights," and pass over into the order of jural relations, but become mutually recognized as such. Whatever there is of International Law and of treaty obligations has thus been gradually brought into being by diplomacy; and together, in their aggregate, imperfect as they are, these results constitute one of the finest and most precious fruits of civilization.

DANGERS ARISING FROM ADVANTAGES IN POSSE

It is important to note that what seems like a valuable "interest" — in the sense of an advantage *in posse* in distinction from a claim *in esse* — is likely to be prematurely identified with a "right" in the mind of the person, or the people, whose mental process has already taken the step of counting it as an asset. This is precisely the kind of object for which human nature is psychologically most predisposed to fight, for it may seem that it is only by fighting that it can be obtained. Plans, hopes, and expectations once treated as realities die very hard; and it is easy for a disappointed person to believe that he has been robbed of that which he has never really possessed. When such experiences are of a public character, when a whole nation, or a turbulent part of it, is impressed with this sense of being disappointed, it requires all the moral strength of firm and intelligent statesmanship to avert the natural result. In such cases, there is seldom a deliberate analysis of facts, a clear application of general principles, or a disposition for delay and examination. The feelings excited seem to justify prompt and violent action, yet this is a time when action is most likely to be of a mistaken nature.

It is in such moments as these, when the public feels that great sacrifices are being made, or that imagined wrongs

THE STATE AND GENERAL WELFARE

should be promptly redressed, that public policy is most difficult; for, in countries where the will of the people is recognized as the standard of action, the temptation of a government to yield to prevailing popular impulse is almost irresistible. It is then that settled and well-tested principles are needed, not only as defining obligations, but for the restraint of precipitate action. As a rule, a state of mind that demands instantaneous satisfaction is a passion rather than a judgment, and in the interest of justice can well bear suspense.

DUTIES OF THE STATE AS A JURISTIC ENTITY

It is the duty of the State, as far as possible, to provide for this kind of situation by laying down general principles beforehand, and devising reasonable methods of procedure. This is precisely what governments have usually been most reluctant to do. They hesitate to limit their own freedom of action, and cherish the idea that, because it is an advantage for the State to maintain its absolute character, it is its right to do so; and, being innocent of harmful intentions in general, this absoluteness cannot be dangerous, they think, to the peace and order of the world. This position is often sustained by the plea, that a government has not the right to leave the State less free than it found it.

There is, at first glance, something seductive about this attitude of refusing to take precautions and to assume obligations. What, it is asked, if the honor of the State should be so involved that it could be defended only by an immediate appeal to arms and the test of battle? Are there not occasions when indignation should be promptly shown, without waiting for discussion?

It is true, that a nation attacked should be in a position to repel the assault promptly, and hence the folly of commending national weakness; for there can be no sound argument against the right of self-defence. Prompt resentment of intended wrong may also sometimes be necessary; but it is rarely the case that it requires bloodshed, and it is usually inexpedient to be hasty in resorting to irrevocable action.

The fundamental question is, what is the duty of a State as a juristic person? Unless we are to return to barbarism, we must always come back to that. And what is the "honor" of a juristic person? Is it not to maintain its juristic character? How can "honor" be better demonstrated than by strictly honorable conduct? And what again is "honor," viewed from the side of its strength, if it is not sufficiently sure of itself to meet its opponents at the testing-place of justice? Why then should a State shrink, in the name of "honor," from giving guarantees for its rectitude of conduct? Why should it not be willing to submit the question of what is honorable, in given circumstances, to those who can fairly measure its aims and motives, and await a verdict?

The truth is, this retreat to the citadel of honor is often a mere subterfuge, intended to cover a previous determination to act in an arbitrary manner. It favors the appeal to force, because it is conscious of moral weakness. Such an attitude is beneath the dignity of the State. Standing as it does for justice against oppression, for law against anarchy, and for reason against violence, it may, without being disturbed by the taunts of cowardice, assume for itself the same precautions and give the same assurances that it commends to those whose conduct it claims the right to govern. It bids the citizen to conform to just laws, to preserve the peace, to carry his grievances before the courts, and to await and respect their decisions. If this be good for citizens, why is not something analogous to it good for States? And, if States impose these requirements upon their constituents, why should they not accept for themselves similar principles, and voluntarily assume corresponding obligations?

THE ALLEGED ESSENTIAL EGOISM OF THE STATE

We are likely at this point, and in answer to these questions, to be reminded, that it would require a revolution in human nature for the State to surrender, or permit to escape, any advantages which it may be able, by virtue of its inherent force, to obtain over others. Engaged with rivals in a struggle for existence, and acting under a natural law which rewards fitness with survival, it is only by the prudent exercise of all its power, it is alleged, that a nation can hope even to maintain its independence. The State must, therefore, exact of all its constituents constant individual sacrifices for the good of the community as a whole; and, in return, it must use all the power thus placed at its disposal for the public benefit.

There is a truth underlying this form of statement, but it requires analysis and exposition to separate it from the erroneous inferences which are often drawn from it. It has required no revolution of human nature to form the Modern State; but it has involved the perception that the natural and ineradicable egoism of the human individual is better served by conformity to certain rules enforced by the State than it was when left to seek satisfaction in conditions of lawlessness.

The transformation which has led to the formation of the Modern State — or we may say to the State in any organized form whatever — has not been accomplished without a long series of struggles and compromises. If we permit ourselves to return in imagination for a moment to the motives in operation in a primitive condition of society, before the State had taken on a definite form and acquired recognized authority, we can readily understand the reluctance with which powerful men laid aside their personal autonomy, and submitted to the supremacy of the State. Being able to defend their own persons and property without the aid of the community, they had no strong motive for submission to any laws imposed by others, even such laws as they might consider as in themselves just. On the other hand, they doubtless found a keen satisfaction in the consciousness of their superior strength, and in their freedom to employ it as they saw fit. They probably felt entire confidence in their ability to judge for themselves what they should do or leave undone, with no restraints upon their volitions. It is also probable, that they experienced a special pride in this condition of irresponsibility to any external power, mingled occasionally perhaps with a fine feeling of being eminently noble and generous in purpose and action. In many instances, no doubt, there was also the reflection, that this personal exemption from authoritative rules, however useful they might be to the community as a whole, afforded to them, as individuals, a career of growing wealth and power which equality before the law would render impossible.

Men of this type were the natural enemies of the State-idea of their time, however rudimentary it may have been, except upon condition that they could employ the State as an instrument for their own advantage. Throughout the whole of historic time, we trace the presence and operation of these motives; sometimes manifesting themselves in open revolt against the State, sometimes in efforts to control and wield its power, and usually in the disposition to treat it as private property when this power was actually possessed.

The Modern State is a triumph, more or less complete, over this opposition to the authority of law. In the time of dynastic predominance, the national monarchies were obliged for a long period to battle with the great feudal lords, who demanded a place almost equal to that of the king, and boldly maintained their right to do so; and it was only through the material force supplied by the people in defence of the more just and liberal decisions of the royal courts that these ambitious pretensions were finally overcome, and the power of the magnates reduced to submission under the reign of law. Finally, it became necessary to bring every form of absolutism within the restraint of law, by the partition of power and the establishment of constitutional guarantees, by which the Modern State was developed as a more faithful guardian of the general welfare.

THE CLASSIC MAXIMS OF DIPLOMACY

However radical the transformation of political power may be, nothing is so difficult as to modify its traditions. Its form may change almost beyond recognition, but its substance inheres in the succession. There has never in human history been a revolution so profound that continuity in this respect has been wholly broken, and the Modern State is not exempt from this inheritance. And yet it is evident, that the idea of the Modern State, which is essentially juristic, is incompatible with a large portion of this inheritance. Existing as it does through the authority of law, it has succeeded but slowly, and as yet imperfectly, in recognizing any law as binding besides its own. As a matter of fact, it is aware of the presence of other nations, and, as we shall presently see, it has gradually come to the recognition of an international society; but it has only in the most recent period been able to conceive of itself, and not yet universally, as essentially a juristic as distinguished from a predatory entity.

As a proof of this, take the assumption, which lies at the foundation of classic diplomacy, that every State is seeking to appropriate for itself everything in the world that possesses value; and is restrained from actually doing so only by the resistance it may encounter.

The great pedagogue of diplomacy, Count de Garden, expresses this fundamental principle in this manner:—
"Every State, in its external relations, has, and can have, no other maxims than these:

"Whoever by the superiority of his forces and by his geographic position can do us harm, is our natural enemy;

"Whoever cannot do us harm, but can, by the extent of his forces and by the position he occupies, do injury to our enemy, is our natural friend." [1]

"These propositions," says Ancillon, "are the pivots upon which all international intercourse turns."

"Fear and distrust" — "indestructible passions," as de Garden calls them — "prolong the state of open or latent war in which the Powers of Europe still live." "The measure of national strength is the only measure of national safety."

Holding firmly to this dogma, that the passion for plunder is not only characteristic of the Modern State, but hope-

---

[1] De Garden, *Tableau Historique de la Diplomatie*, Paris; and *Histoire Générale des Traités de Paix*, Paris, I, Introduction.

lessly ineradicable, many diplomatists and statesmen who count themselves strictly orthodox still affect to regard jurisprudence as mere ideology. They consider it impossible to establish any other permanent relations between States than those of mutual fear and distrust; which have, they claim, always existed between nations, and must exist forever. They hold that history confirms their doctrine; and that States, in whatever form they have existed, are mere temporary and local means for repressing within themselves the aggressive and avaricious instincts of human nature; and that these instincts are destined forever to break forth in some new form of ferocity and destruction, unless they are held firmly in the leash by the hand of power. Statesmen of this school of thought have little faith in any form of self-government, regard the idea of justice as a purely abstract and unrealizable ideal, and consider law as a more or less arbitrary restraint upon the mass, imposed by great masters, against whose authority the natural man is in an attitude of endless secret revolt.

Experience, it is said, furnishes overwhelming proof of this doctrine. Kingdoms, empires, and even republics have been born, flourished, languished, and died without ever forming a permanent international society based upon the idea of law and reciprocal obligation. The nomad warriors who finally established their dominions in Assyria, Medea, and Persia were obliged to build upon foundations of centralized despotism, and to maintain their empires by force alone. When, after ferocious wars, ending in the triumph of the stronger, luxury and self-indulgence sapped their military virtues, and other warriors more fierce and hardy fell upon them, their power was swept away, and passed into the possession of the conqueror.

The commercial nations of a later date that for a time controlled the destinies of the Mediterranean built their splendor upon the idea of wealth; but they also disappeared, yielding to greater valor, leaving behind them the traditions of "Phoenician fraud" and "Punic faith."

The quasi-republican States of Greece, long engaged in recurrent quarrels for hegemony, finally rose to the conception of an Amphictyonic and an Achaean League; but the former was merely a religious fraternity intended for the preservation of the oracle at Delphi, and the latter was only a feeble alliance of too slight a nature to withstand the assault of a military superior.

And all these examples, it is contended, only illustrate the essentially unstable character of the State, its constant exposure to extinction, and its certain doom when its military vigor and expansive policies are relaxed.

THE NEW ELEMENT IN THE MODERN STATE

But in all this reasoning the new and determinative element in the Modern State is overlooked. As we have seen, that element is the wide-spread development of jural consciousness nourished and strengthened by the experience of living under a progressive constitutional régime, which has demonstrated the practical advantages of the reign of law over existence dominated by arbitrary force. It is not necessary to prove that human nature has changed, or will change, or that men are in any degree less self-regarding or inspired by a loftier altruism than prevailed in former times. It is simply that humanity has discovered a new path, and is disposed to follow it. It is perceived that happiness can be obtained more easily and more surely by industry than by plunder, by commerce than by piracy, by intercourse between the nations than by isolation. It is, therefore, necessary to reckon with the new social forces and the new standards of conduct that have come into being through improved transportation, practically instantaneous communication, the discovery of new natural resources, and of new forms of energy to render them available.

It is important to consider also, that the Modern State, affording more equal opportunities, and covering productive effort with the aegis of its protection, has changed the whole nature of society. The individual is probably no less egoistic than before, but new avenues of profitable activity are opened to his enterprise. The age of *condottieri* and of mercenary troops is passed. The citizen-soldier does not look forward to the spoils of war as the dream of his existence. International spoliation has ceased to be a trade. Yet all the old traditions of depredations from beyond the border, of peaceful commerce exposed to capture at sea, of crushing indemnities to be paid by the vanquished to the invading conqueror are kept alive, and serve to thrill the readers of sensational publications, and to enforce the assent of parliamentary committees to extravagant military appropriations. "Fear and distrust," the "natural enemy" just across the frontier, the secret treaties suspected to exist between our neighbors, — all these linger on, — creating the mirage of terror and suspicion that fills the sky only because there is a background of mist on which alarming images are painted by a sun that has set!

"But no," it will be said, "the light of yesterday has not departed. These fears are well grounded. Our natural enemy is stronger than we; and he will, therefore, avenge himself upon us." Acting upon this assurance, we strive to become stronger than he; and now this "natural enemy" says, with all honesty, "An assault is imminent. We must prepare to resist it." And so, by a process of endless circular reasoning, the illusion of hatred and hostility is kept alive.

It seems rather remarkable, that governments, who should be the first to dispel this illusion, are the most belated of all in perceiving that great changes have taken place in the relations of peoples. Across the frontier there is another civilized people, with a jural consciousness as deep, as enlightened, and as anxious as our own. We loan them, or they loan us, vast sums of money; exchanging hundreds of millions of dollars of securities, on the faith of our railroads, our municipalities, even of our governments. Will these debts ever be paid? In the time when our nearest neighbor, stronger than we, was really our "natural enemy," and really would have invaded our territory and annexed us, securities and all, it is doubtful if they would have been paid; but no one now doubts that they will be. Bankers do not doubt it, investors do not doubt it; why then should governments believe, that these same people, who expect to pay their debts, are meditating invasion and conquest, with all that they imply? Simply because they have no serious assurance to the contrary.

And so it happens, that the Modern State, the embodiment of law and the protagonist of justice, whose simple promise to pay is bought by the million in the open market by the shrewdest interpreters of human intentions, — the bankers and money-lenders, — permits itself to be discredited by a dogma of diplomacy which sounds to every honest man like a calumny on human decency.

THE NEED OF GUARANTEES OF JUSTICE

It is, of course, evident, that the ground of general "fear and distrust" is the conviction that Modern States are, in reality, not juristic but predatory entities; and, it must be confessed, that they have taken little pains to prove that they are not. To change this conviction, but one thing is needed, namely: a sufficiently guaranteed assurance that the State will be just. It is not so important to demand that the capacity to inflict injury be diminished; for a Great Power, however much it might reduce its immediately effective strength, would still be formidable, if it afterward decided for any reason to increase its military effectiveness; and a demand that a State should weaken itself to diminish our fears would imply, that, after all, it is the possession of power, and not the use to be made of it, which constitutes the great source of international danger. The only permanent assurance of just intentions on the part of governments is their frank and loyal acceptance of the juristic character of the State, supported by evidence that they have the same interest in justice abroad that they have at home.

It may be felt, that if the State did not place the rights and interests of its own constituents above the rights of foreigners, it would lose its hold upon its own people; and that, unless it were more or less chauvinistic in its policies, patriotism would be displaced by resentment of the State's indifference. But this is an ill-calculated apprehension. Universal welfare does not diminish local welfare; it only places a new value upon it; and enriches each by the greater prosperity of all. Every man's rights are rendered more secure by the increased security of all rights. A world of universal law and order would be a safer, a more useful, and a more valuable world to every man living in it than a world where arbitrary force and injustice somewhere prevail. The integrity of the State as regards the welfare of its constituents would be powerfully strengthened by perfect integrity in its outward relations, and every effort to render it more just and honorable would reinforce the respect and devotion with which it is regarded by those upon whose loyalty it must depend.

What is true of the State as an institution is true also of its policies. It is impossible for a government that deals falsely or unjustly abroad to awaken pride or inspire confidence at home. A refusal to submit to principles of equity weakens the very foundations of the State; for men do not need to be told, that those who are ready to wrong others in the interest of their country will in their own interest be ready to wrong their countrymen when they have the opportunity to do so.

It is then not only in keeping with the essential aim and purpose of the State, but of highest importance to its own welfare, that there should be no pretence of exemption from the great principles of jurisprudence to which it appeals when it claims obedience. Its real strength, as well as its dignity, lies in the maintenance of its juristic character; for it is in and through this character that it has the right to command. We cheerfully yield to it our loyal obedience; not because it has power, but because it is the embodiment of justice. We may then rightly demand, that the State shall itself be just; and that it shall both seek and grant effective guarantees that justice shall prevail in the society of States.

IV

THE STATE AS A MEMBER OF A SOCIETY

WE have seen that the Modern State contains elements which separate it widely from the governmental institutions of an earlier period, and have prepared it for relations of a different character from those that formerly prevailed. It is also worthy of special attention, that it is only in comparatively recent times that States have regarded themselves as belonging to an international society in which they possess a jural equality.

The bearing of these changes upon the problem of world organization is so important, that it may be profitable to review briefly the circumstances which have produced this condition. It may be well also to recall the fact, that, long before the Modern State came into being, the nations which have developed it belonged, for the greater part, to one self-conscious community, under the name of Christendom.

That form of culture which we call "civilization" was derived from the influence of the Roman Empire upon those portions of Europe, Asia, and Africa over which the rule of Rome extended its dominion. After the fall of the Empire, it was to Rome in the West, and to Byzantium in the East, that Europe looked for the renewal and extention of those cultural influences which had so largely transformed the barbarian tribes subdued by Roman conquests, and which did not entirely fail to command respect when the barbarian kings partitioned the territories of the Empire, and set up upon its soil their independent kingdoms.

THE UNIFYING INFLUENCES OF THE CHURCH

When, through internal corruption and diminished vitality, the Roman Empire fell, it was superseded by a dominion of souls even wider in extent; and a spiritual empire lived on in the minds of men long after Rome's political dismemberment. Powerful and persistent as Roman Law proved to be, the Church was vastly more influential, and by its triumph over the rude instincts of the barbaric invaders placed the stamp of its unity upon the whole of Western and Northern Europe. All the barbarian kings eventually became sons of the same foster mother, the Church at Rome, and bowed with reverence before her altar.

The significance of this for the future of mankind can hardly be adequately estimated. Notwithstanding the hostility of races and the fiery ambitions of their leaders, every individual in the wide expanse of Western Christendom had a sense of membership in a universal community. The most potent sentiments of human nature were touched and swayed by a common symbol, — the sign of the cross. All that was sacred in life was connected with it; and birth, life, and death paid tribute to it. Dominated by its power and its mystery, all men at all stages of their existence felt the pressure of its authority, and accepted the brotherhood it conferred upon them all.

We have very superficially studied the Middle Ages, if we have failed to appreciate the strength of this common bond. Throughout that long period of deplorable ignorance and turbulent passion, when all that was noblest and all that was basest in human nature were in a state of conflict, rendered inevitable by the sudden mixture of motives and an imperfect social organization, the general sense of community was never lost. Bred to battle, and harried by the invasion of fresh hordes of barbarians, as yet untempered by the thought of mercy, princes and peoples often strove heroically to live according to the Law of Christ. The few pages of our histories relating to that time are filled chiefly with accounts of private and feudal wars; but they take little notice of the gentle deeds, the noble sacrifices, the sublime renunciations, and the peaceful and tranquil years and decades that filled those eight centuries of human existence. We speak superciliously of things "medieval," of which for the most part we are wholly ignorant; but we overlook the lofty personal aspirations after good and the humble sense of universal brotherhood that made those long centuries appear so brief in history, and yet rendered them so rich in influence upon the transformation of mankind. It is only when we behold the visible monuments of their love and sacrifice, when we visit the churches and cathedrals which remain as memorials of their skill, their sense of beauty, and their conscientious fidelity in workmanship, that we catch some faint idea of the feeling that possessed those men for the invisible kingdom, not of this world, which in their faith bound all men together in one vast and permanent fellowship of souls.

Of a direct legal relation between sovereign princes, outside of the feudal system, — which was based upon the idea of a graded community, — we find in the literature of the Middle Ages but little consciousness. Separate kingdoms and principalities they knew, but the sense of unity was so deep and so overwhelming, that the idea of distinct and reciprocal relations between them was difficult to form. Within the circle of Christendom, the bond of relation, moral or legal, was not so much between themselves as with the higher powers, to which they were all in common subjected. In the days of faith, the quarrels of kings and princes were taken to the judgment-seat of Rome, and the intervention and decision of the Holy Father were reverently invoked. In the majority of cases, that decision, pronounced by the Pope, or mediated through his legates, was respected and obeyed. It is true, that the long and tragic conflict between the Empire and the Papacy was a struggle constantly renewed; but through it all the spiritual community remained substantially unbroken. It was not until the controversies of Boniface VIII with the national monarchs, and the transfer of the papal throne to Avignon, in 1305, that the sense of unity was lost. Then began a process of mutual alienation that culminated in the Great Schism of 1378, which ended the unity of Christendom in Western Europe. Thereafter, the decisions of Rome were habitually disregarded, and finally repudiated altogether.

It was not, however, until the Protestant Reformation had divided Christendom into two permanently hostile camps, that attention was directed to the existence of a natural community of nations which required them to be regarded as forming a society in which they were directly bound together by moral and legal obligations. It was then attempted, since the bond of a common religious faith had been broken, to find a new basis for the restoration of that unity which had before prevailed. In the meantime, States in the modern sense had begun to come into existence, and the fact could not long escape observation.

THE STATE AS A MEMBER OF A SOCIETY

SUAREZ' RECOGNITION OF THE SOCIETY OF STATES

The first writer to call explicit attention to the existence of a society of States governed by jural laws was the Portuguese theologian, Franciscus Suarez (1548–1617), who has been called "the last of the Schoolmen." In a passage of singular clearness and depth of insight, Suarez wrote: "The human race, however divided into various peoples and kingdoms, has always not only its unity as a species but also a certain moral and quasi-political unity, pointed out by the natural precepts of mutual love and pity, which extends to all, even to foreigners of any nation. Wherefore, although every perfect State, whether a republic or a kingdom, is in itself a perfect community composed of its own members, still each such State, viewed in relation to the human race, is in some measure a member of that universal unity. For those communities are never singly so self-sufficing but that they stand in need of some mutual aid, society, and communion, sometimes for the improvement of their condition and their greater convenience, — but sometimes also for their moral necessity and need, as appears by experience. For that reason, they are in need of some law by which they may be directed and rightly ordered in that kind of communion and society. And, although this is to a great extent supplied by natural reason, yet it is not so supplied sufficiently and immediately for all purposes; and, therefore, it has been possible for particular laws to be introduced by the practice of those nations. For just as custom introduced law in a State or province, so it was possible for laws to be introduced in the whole human race by the habitual conduct of nations; and that all the more, because the points which belong to this law are few, and approach very nearly to natural law;

and, being easily deduced from it, are useful and agreeable to nature; so that, although this law cannot be plainly deduced as being altogether necessary in itself to laudable conduct, still it is very suitable to nature, and such as all may accept for its own sake." [1]

Thus, as early as 1612, when the work of Suarez was published, note was taken of the fact that nations did not exist in isolation, or without a certain interdependence and reciprocity of obligation, both moral and legal; for custom had unconsciously created laws, which they recognized as possessing utility. Even before this, the Spanish judge-advocate Balthazar Ayala (1548–1584), treating of the just causes of war, had in 1581 referred to "the laudable and ancient customs introduced between Christians," thus indirectly recognizing the existence of a society of States governed by law; and Albericus Gentilis (1551–1608), professor of the Civil Law at Oxford, writing upon the same subject in 1585, had discerned a foundation for law in the "consent" of nations.

The Modern State, the embodiment of law, was at that time very imperfectly formed; but the jural consciousness of nations was already beginning to be developed, and it was a mark of keen observation on the part of Suarez to perceive that a society of States had already come into existence; but his range of knowledge was not sufficient to enable him to define with accuracy the limits of that society. In making it universal, he overshot the facts as they then existed, but rendered the great service of indicating the essential unity of mankind as a ground for an ever growing social recognition.

In one respect, Suarez was far in advance of his time, and three centuries have hardly overtaken him. A Catholic in religion, he saw no barrier in race to membership in the

[1] Suarez, *Tractatus de Legibus et Deo Legislatore*, Coimbra, 1612.

universal society of mankind. For him, whenever organized States came into being, there could be no obstacle to treating them with equity and admitting them to equal participation in the common Law of Nations. A sense of community which had gradually extended the boundaries of Christendom over the barbarian world, and gathered its scattered tribes into the fold of the Universal Church, could not comprehend the existence of limits to the society of nations, so long as anything human remained to be brought within its fellowship.

THE OUTLAWRY OF THE STRANGER IN PRIMITIVE TIMES

In the early period of Rome, whose imperial law was eventually extended over parts of three continents, and, as the limits of the Empire widened, was considered more and more adapted to be made universal, jural law, as distinguished from moral law, was not regarded as applicable to all persons within its territory.

"It is throughout a modern idea," says the latest authority on the history of the law of aliens, "that law should be made an international benefit; and the position that prevails to-day is as remote as the heavens from that of antiquity. In that age, the State and all it commanded existed only for the citizen, including both law and religion. He who was not a citizen possessed no jural right. The individual was assigned to his State, and could not leave it without surrendering his personal *status* and becoming a homeless man, possessing no legal rights. From this arose the dread of exile in antiquity."[1]

In primitive times, the alien was everywhere considered not only as devoid of legal rights, but also as not even entitled to the protection of his life. Without doubt, there al-

[1] Frisch, *Das Fremdenrecht*, p. 3.

ways existed a certain respect for the person of the innocent stranger, and hospitality was not of necessity denied him; although the earliest tendency was to regard the stranger as also an enemy. Of this there remains a vestige in the relationship between the Latin words *hospes*, guest, and *hostis*, enemy.[1] But legally, according either to the customary or written laws, the stranger stood apart, and was sharply discriminated from members of the community.

We are able to trace with considerable precision the changes which occurred in this respect; and it is important to note these modifications, for they offer an explanation of the fact that, while the laws of all modern civilized nations explicitly recognize the rights of strangers, yet in the minds of the masses of the people, there is still a clear discrimination made between citizens and foreigners; and not unfrequently there is a feeling that the rights of the stranger are less entitled to consideration, particularly in economic relations, than those of residents; and this is more observable in small communities, where the presence of strangers is less frequent.

In the earliest times, the alien, being without legal rights, could legally be made a slave; and was often retained for that purpose. It is interesting to notice, that, in the treaties between the small city-states of Greece, in the fifth century before our era, the right of asylum plays a great part; indicating the necessity that then existed of securing by special conventions the protection of persons travelling or residing in foreign lands.

Later, we find in Greece a class of persons called *proxenoi*, charged with the protection of strangers, and performing functions analogous to those of our modern consuls, especially in

---

[1] See, however, Phillipson, *The International Law and Custom of Ancient Greece and Rome*, London, 1911, pp. 215, 216.

the orient, where the right of extraterritoriality is still recognized. Indeed, we may see in this arrangement a survival of the ancient idea that the stranger possessed no rights under the laws of a foreign country, attended with the even older idea that law is personal rather than territorial, which prevailed of necessity among all nomad tribes and continued to persist long after the time when the great migrations ended. And this enables us to understand how a people remaining nearer in their conceptions of law to its primitive forms and conditions finds it possible, without violence to its ideas of right, to permit the presence of what is in reality a foreign jurisdiction, which to us, familiar only with uniform law within a given territory, would be intolerable.

THE GRADUAL RECOGNITION OF THE STRANGER'S RIGHTS

At Rome, for a long time, the foreigner possessed no legal rights except those that belonged to captives under the laws of war, which did not prevent reducing him to slavery. Gradually, however, there grew up in the jural consciousness of the Romans the institution of *hospitium*, by which a Roman, acting in the quality of friend, could take the foreigner under his protection as a guest, and cover him temporarily with the mantle of his own rights as a citizen; but, even in this case, the stranger had no right of his own, and could not only be abandoned by his host, but could be legally treated by him as if he were an enemy.

Finally, *hospitium* took on a public character at Rome, and the stranger was accorded a legal right of residence, under the law represented by his person, especially if his country had secured it for him by treaty; and he was then judged by the *praetor perigrinus* under the *Jus Gentium*. It was not until the year 212 of our era, when Caracalla accorded the right of citizenship to all free inhabitants of the Empire, that the stranger was at last able to obtain for himself the full rights of a Roman citizen.[1]

Among the Germanic tribes, the original conception of law was "*Verbandsrecht*," that is, a rule of right growing out of some kind of special tie, or bond, between persons. For every family, every mark, there was a law, to which all outside of it were strangers. When, later, conditions required an extension of the idea of law, the conception took the form of different laws for different forms of union or relationship; but still applicable only to the membership of a definite group. Christianity and Roman influence gradually made themselves felt among the Germanic peoples, and in time they came to recognize their participation in the greater community of Christendom, but always more from a moral or spiritual than from a legal point of view. Charles the Great ordained by a general law, — although he had adopted personal law as the main principle of his empire, — that no one should deny to the stranger "roof, fire, and water." Other more local Germanic laws required that the stranger be allowed pasture for his horse, to build a fire, to pluck a certain quantity of fruit and catch a certain quantity of fish, and to cut enough wood to repair his wagon. In practice, Tacitus says, that the hospitality of the Germans — meaning thereby not the right but the usage — surpasses that of all other peoples; and it continues to do so to this day. But the *rights* of the stranger have been but slowly recognized by all nations of Germanic origin. We speak now not of the people of Germany, but

[1] The question whether Caracalla's gift of the Roman franchise changed the personal law is a subject of controversy. Phillipson, before cited, pp. 281, 282. Walker, *History of the Law of Nations*, Cambridge, 1899, I, pp. 119, 120.

of the Germanic race in all its branches; for, until comparatively recent times, its idea of law was rooted and grounded in custom, — the custom of the family, of the local community, and of the particular class or group to which law may be applied. In general, the Germanic mind distrusts abstract ideas, abstract reasoning, and abstract generalizations; it lives in the concrete, in realities, and in their immediate conditions and consequences. It is not that the Germanic type of mind is less just, and it is in practice perhaps even the most generous; it is rather that it is constitutionally indisposed to bind and restrict its perfect freedom of action by any unnecessary forms of restraint. Add to this the characteristic Germanic consciousness of inexhaustible vigor, which furnishes the basis of self-reliance, and the difficulty it has of considering any other race quite equal to itself, and it is evident why, as a race, it has always wished to make its own laws, has been proud of them when they have been made, and has had less interest in human society as a totality of civilized men than it has had in taking a preëminent, and even a predominating, place in that society.

THE DEVELOPMENT OF SELF-CONSCIOUSNESS IN THE SOCIETY OF STATES

It has seemed profitable to dwell somewhat upon the attitude of the local community toward the individual stranger as regards his jural character, because it enables us to understand more clearly why the separate Sovereign States of Europe were so slow in learning to recognize one another as possessing the same reciprocal jural rights, and in developing in themselves the consciousness that such a society existed, and that they were responsible members of it.

It was, quite naturally, in the maritime countries, where foreign trade was developed, that the stranger found most consideration; partly perhaps because there was an advantage in his presence. He was usually protected in life and limb, and often allowed to sue in the ordinary courts. Sometimes he was placed under the care of a native host, and granted a jury that could understand his language. As Professor Walker has said, in his "History of the Law of Nations," "He was a 'man of the Emperor,' or a Hanseatic merchant, and the king received him gladly, though native traders might growl their hate, and native apprentices while away a happy holiday in sacking his well-stored steelyard. Or, again, while defended by the local ruler from the attacks of others, he was taxed and pillaged by that ruler himself in every conceivable fashion, and on every conceivable pretext: he came to claim the heritage of a deceased ancestor, and he was fined by the monarch in virtue of a *droit de détraction;* he was a Jew or a Lombard, and he became the royal sponge, paying for the privilege of extracting usury from the people by the privilege of providing for the extravagances of the king: he resided in his special Jewry and his Lombard Street, and his moneybags furnished the bankrupt local royal exchequer under the telling inducements of the hangman's whip or the niceties of torture; he might be at any time expelled by the tyrant, but if, his wrath provoked by some unusual outrage, he strove to withdraw, he might find himself obliged to purchase permission so to remove with his goods by the payment of a *gabelle* (*droit d'émigration*); and, should he at last die a stranger in a strange land, it commonly happened that the vultures of the Crown swooped down once more and robbed the alien heir under the name of the *droit d'aubaine.*" [1]

[1] Walker, *History of the Law of Nations*, Cambridge, 1899, I, pp. 119, 120.

Of these impositions upon the foreigner, the *droit d'aubaine* was one of the most unjust and one of the most tenacious, having been abolished in some countries only as late as the end of the eighteenth century. It consisted in the alleged right of a monarch to confiscate the whole estate of a foreigner dying upon his territory. In England, particular lords had this right with regard to their domains. It was usual to forbid foreigners to own real estate, but this did not prevent the entire loss of personal property.

If the individual stranger had no adequate security for his property under the laws of the foreign country, what could be expected from it in relation to the natural rights of another State? Evidently, nothing which it could not obtain by force of arms. The society of States was, therefore, regarded as a society existing in a "state of nature." As late as 1651, when his book called "Leviathan" appeared, Thomas Hobbes wrote: "In all places, where men have lived by small families, to rob and spoil one another has been a trade, and so far from being reputed against the Law of Nature, the greater spoils they gained, the greater was their honor." And to show that he was not describing merely the practices of some primitive age, he adds: "As small families did then, so now do cities and kingdoms, which are greater families, for their own security enlarge their dominions upon all pretences of danger and fear of invasion . . . endeavoring, as much as they can, to subdue by open force or secret arts, for want of other caution, justly; and are remembered for it in after years with honor." [1]

When we consider that these words were written by a famous English philosopher a quarter of a century after Grotius had composed his great work on "The Rights of War

[1] Hobbes, *Leviathan*, Chapters XIII and XVII.

and Peace," we may be able to realize to what small extent the jural consciousness of nations had at that time included the relations between Sovereign States.

Still, the fact of the existence of such a society was beginning to be firmly grasped and becoming a more frequent object of reflection. It was, indeed, conceived as existing in a "state of nature," with war and plunder as its most salient features; but it was something that it was being considered at all, for it only needed to be made the subject of examination to quicken the jural consciousness of nations to a new life.

As Professor Sidgwick has well pointed out in his book on "The Development of European Polity," "In the Middle Ages, it was recognized that everyone has rights, and this was a step toward legality. But it was in the nature of that time that, when a dispute arose between neighbors, no one was sure of getting his rights; because there was no one to settle the dispute, and it had to be fought out by the contestants."[1] The characteristic of the Modern State is, that it is possible in it to find what the law is, and to apply it, without actually fighting for justice. And it was already becoming apparent in the middle of the seventeenth century that Sovereign States have rights also, and that laws were needed, if they did not already exist, by which those rights might be recognized and protected; but, in the absence of any clear statement of those laws, or power to enforce them, the society of States was still perturbed by almost continual disorder and violence, despoiled by plunder, and devasted by war. It was a painful consciousness to which Europe was awakening, but it proved to be a birth into a new world.

[1] Sidgwick, *The Development of European Polity*, London, 1903, p. 324.

THE THIRTY YEARS' WAR AND THE PEACE OF WESTPHALIA

The progress of mankind is often accomplished through a deep sense of its own imperfections. It frequently happens, therefore, that the contemplation of a degenerate age gives rise to a profound revulsion of feeling and a sober and earnest endeavor to reconstitute the social order.

The Thirty Years' War, which began with the Bohemian revolution in 1618 and terminated with the Peace of Westphalia, marked the lowest state of degradation to which Europe had descended since the time of primitive barbarism. In that desperate conflict, the basest passions mingled with the noblest purposes and the most heroic sacrifices in the effort to settle by brute force questions of the deepest moral and religious significance. A hireling soldiery, ready to fight for pay under any standard, making war its profession, sacked populous cities, murdered the inhabitants, devastated a great part of Central Europe, and left behind it a scene of ruin, suffering, and desolation which centuries were required to repair. Multitudes were homeless, two-thirds of the houses in Germany having been destroyed; yet so great was the loss of life that only half the remainder were occupied. An entire generation had known little but tales of slaughter; and war, in its most brutal and disgusting forms, had come to appear to those who in their entire lives had witnessed nothing else as the natural and permanent condition of mankind.

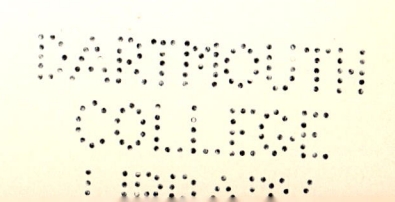

It was in the midst of these terrific occurrences that both Grotius and Hobbes formed their views of the nature of society. Both were confronted with the same facts, but they saw in them very different meanings. For Hobbes, the picture of nations living "in a condition of perpetual war and upon the confines of battle" represented the permanent reality with which the statesman and the political philosopher have to deal. A realist to the core, Hobbes declared in his pitiless frankness that, being a perpetual prey to the rapacity of others, the life of man, while he continues to live in a state of nature, will doubtless always be "solitary, poor, nasty, brutish, and short"; but, nevertheless, he says, "this is his natural condition." Needing for his happiness above all peace, there is only one chance of obtaining it; and that is to obey and support a government strong enough to secure it to him, as the reward for his willing obedience to its supreme commands. The only hope of mankind is, therefore, in absolute government, through which men can so associate themselves with power that they may share the portion of its advantages that may be accorded to them, and at least be saved from plunder and murder by their foes.

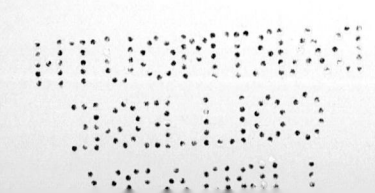

For Grotius, the same picture of brutal struggle had quite an opposite meaning. He saw in it not a natural, but an unnatural, condition of human society, utterly repulsive to his own nature. He perceived that men are endowed with faculties which mere brutes do not possess, that these faculties are not the accidents but the distinctive characteristics of man as a species, and that the normal exercise of them would preserve society from these terrific orgies of devastation and bloodshed which spring from the unsuppressed and unregulated explosions of man's lower instincts. There was, in his view, something in common between the contestants on both sides of the savage conflict between religious opinions, — a common faith in a higher power, as well as a common faculty of reason, which nature had bestowed upon all men as a bond of union between them. It could not be then that war was to be perpetual, and that war itself, if really necessary for a just cause, should not be conducted according to principles implanted in the better nature of man.

The Peace of Westphalia, the negotiations for which covered eleven years and were interrupted by repeated renewals of the war, finally proved that Grotius was right. When both sides were exhausted, and the Congress of Westphalia had for more than five years wrangled over the terms of settlement, on October 24, 1648, the treaties of peace were signed simultaneously at Münster and Osnabrück.

THE SIGNIFICANCE OF THE PEACE OF WESTPHALIA

The Peace of Westphalia was not the recognition of any individual right, and cannot be celebrated as the triumph of personal religious freedom. It was, both in form and in substance, a compact between Sovereign Powers, by which each recognized the right of the others to regulate the affairs of religion within their own territories. Regarded from this point of view, it was the last act in the destruction of that formal unity which had once prevailed in Western Europe. But it was not preëminently a destructive change. It was constructive in several important respects. First of all, it ended forever both the political and spiritual aspirations after universal empire. It distinctly recognized a society of States based upon the principle of territorial sovereignty, and settled the doctrine, that law goes with the land, and that each territorial State is independent and possessed of jural rights which all others are bound to respect. It was thus a declaration, not only that a society of States exists, but that it is based on law, is governed by law, and that its members may make their appeal to law. What is most important of all perhaps is the equal recognition of all forms of government without distinction. The Venetian Oligarchy, the

Dutch Republic, the Swiss Confederation, and the Hanseatic Cities were all embraced in it with the same legal rights as the proudest and most ancient monarchies, including the Holy Roman Empire. Practically all the Christian States of Europe, not excepting the Grand Duchy of Moscovy, were embraced within its provisions. Only the Ottoman Empire was excluded from it. It created a Magna Charta for the society of European States, and gave it for the first time a really jural existence. Although the papal nuncio Chigi had served as a mediator at Osnabrück, Innocent X protested against the treaties as "perpetually null, vain, wicked, and . . . without force and effect"; but both Catholics and Protestants alike accepted them as constituting the fundamental law of Europe; and Mathieu Molé, addressing the King of France, referred to the Peace in terms of reverence as *"l'ouvrage du ciel et non des hommes."*

It was, no doubt, too much to expect, that a society which had been engaged in hostilities not only for thirty, but for hundreds of years, the members of which were rent by domestic quarrels and some of them by civil war, would immediately change its character and continue without interruption the work of general pacification and orderly development of its jural relations. But the Peace of Westphalia may be rightly regarded as opening a new era in the history of mankind. Still, it is not possible to overlook the fact, that it contributed additional momentum to the forces that were working for the growth of absolutism in the State. It aided to intensify the self-consciousness of the State, and to render governments more alert, more centralized, and more powerful than they ever had been before. It is only by a careful study of the Age of Absolutism, which covers the period following the Peace of Westphalia to the Revolutionary

Era, that we can comprehend the full significance of that Peace. The old order of attempted reconciliation between spiritual ideals and material interests had passed away with the Wars of Religion, and a new consciousness of material advantages to be gained, and of power to pursue them, supervened. It was the age of the *Grand Monarch*, of the quest for new kingdoms, of diplomatic intrigue, and political adventure, in which the old religious impulsions and restraints played little part. The personal sovereign became the centre of interest, his court the hot-bed of vice and of schemes to support it, and the people the prey to theories invented to glorify the throne and bind them to the dangerous task of rendering it supreme.

THE INFLUENCE OF NEW THEORIES OF GOVERNMENT UPON THE SOCIETY OF STATES

In this respect, Hobbes also had his triumph. It was his philosophy which took the lead in moulding the immediate destinies of the State. It is true, that his idea of the necessity of absolute government contained an explicit qualification, — a qualification which at a later time played an important rôle in justifying revolution, — namely, that a man's obedience to a government, while it should be implicit and unquestioning, may and should end when that government is no longer able to protect his interests. But this only reveals the crude materialism on which the whole system of Hobbes reposes. For him, government is founded upon a "compact" between a subject and a sovereign, by the terms of which the subject agrees to support the sovereign, and to obey him absolutely, so long as the sovereign secures to him the *interests* for which the compact was made.

The effect of such a doctrine upon the society of States can be easily imagined. The State being, in its essence, upon this theory, merely a mutual benefit association, the subject is served best by the success of the State as a predatory enterprise by which others are despoiled; and war, which in a "state of nature," according to Hobbes, is universal and perpetual, having been suppressed within the State for the benefit of its subjects, will very naturally, and, as Hobbes does not hesitate to say, quite "justly," continue its natural course between States, which have no such "compact" with a superior power to preserve them from its evils. Law and order, therefore, upon the theory of Hobbes, end with the particular State. Internationally, since political society is founded upon "*interests*," and not upon "*rights*," — which with Machiavelli he does not recognize as inherent in the nature of man, — war will go on indefinitely, since there is no way of stopping it, and that nation will be the best off which, being the strongest, can most despoil the rest.

It is reasonable to expect that a Society of States in which this philosophy prevails will hardly find the moral law sufficient to preserve the peace. Whether taken directly from Hobbes or from other sources, it was in substance the system of thought by which the Age of Absolutism was practically governed in the relations of States to one another; and the theory upon which it is grounded cannot be said to have been entirely abandoned even in the most modern times.

It was not long, however, before the consequences of such a theory of government as Hobbes propounded were plainly visible in their effect upon society within the State. An absolute government was found to be so burdensome as to be intolerable. The first to expose its imperfections and substitute for the ideas upon which it rested a different theory was John Locke (1632–1704). In his "Treatise on Civil Government," published in 1689, he also based his teaching upon a "compact," — like that of Hobbes, — historically, of course, a fiction, but serving well for purposes of exposition. For Locke, however, government was not originally created by an agreement for the protection of "interests," but for the defence of "rights." Every man, says Locke, in a "state of nature" possesses *rights*, — the right to his life, to exemption from personal injury, and to the peaceable possession of his property. While he remains in the "state of nature" he can secure these rights only by defending them himself, and this perhaps imperfectly. Men have, therefore, combined to found civil society, instituted for the purpose of protecting their rights, and have established governments to afford them protection. They have in no respect surrendered their rights, which they retain in their completeness; but, in exchange for the protection they receive, they have promised to obey and support the government they have established; which they are bound to do so long as the government faithfully defends the rights which it has undertaken to protect, and no longer. In brief, a government derives its authority from a "constitution," — which Locke conceived of as unwritten; — and when this constitution is violated the government created by it is ended, and men are free to establish another, if they choose, in a different form.

The bearing of this theory upon the society of States is evident, though it was no part of Locke's purpose to apply it to international affairs. If the single State rests upon a "compact," there is no reason why a group or association of States should not rest upon a compact also; and, therefore, form a society of States in the same jural sense that a single State is an organized society of men.

But the theory of Locke carries us a step farther. It is not necessary to the substantial correctness of his doctrine that at any particular moment of historic time men should have passed from a "state of nature" by assembling together and making an agreement to form a State. If there ever was such a moment, which is improbable, thousands of generations of men have existed since that time, and these have not formally made such a contract. The most that can be said is, that these, born into a State already existing, have tacitly accepted the terms of a compact actually in force.

Considered from this point of view, in the final analysis, the true foundation of the State and of its government is "the *consent* of the governed"; assuming that they are capable of expressing their consent.

THE EFFECT OF LOCKE'S DOCTRINE ON THE CONCEPTION OF SOVEREIGNTY

It is not difficult to perceive to what conclusions this doctrine leads as to the true conception of sovereignty, and also as to where sovereignty ultimately resides.

First of all, it recognizes no idea of sovereign power that is not based on inherent natural rights. The State, therefore, cannot be above rights, or supreme over rights, in any sense whatever; since it is itself the creature of rights, which are its only source of authority. If it were mere *power*, not based on rights, it would require some other origin than this theory ascribes to it.

It is true, the State possesses power, and power to enforce obedience; but it is a grant supplied and surrendered to the use of government by those who furnish it, as an instrument for the defence of their rights; and when it is used for any other purpose, the original grantors may rightly, according to the compact, refuse to replenish it, may oppose it, and if necessary may restrain it by force.

There is, however, at this point, one qualification to be made. The State cannot be considered as having at any past time been completely and unalterably constituted. It is not an entirely closed compact, incapable of modification. It is, of necessity, a development. It is forever alterable by law, because it is the embodiment of law; and new laws may continue to be made, as long as the law-making power keeps within the limits of the original "compact" to provide for the protection of rights. But from this it appears to follow, that, when laws have once been made, and consent to them has been given, in the form ordained by the "compact," they are binding upon all, and the power of the State may be rightly employed to enforce them.

Thus conceived, sovereignty is nothing else than the right of free self-determination possessed by the State as a juristic person. To speak of it as "supreme above all law," is to misrepresent its true nature; for it is an assertion of law-ordained capacity. Apart from law, it has no meaning. An aggregation of men not associated for jural purposes, and not bound to obey laws, could not possibly be regarded as forming a State; no matter how large or how powerful that association might be. A predatory band, organized for plunder, or a company of merchants organized solely for trade, do not constitute a State, even though it may be equipped with artillery and armed vessels as a means of compelling conformity to its will. The whole specific content of sovereign authority consists, therefore, in its jural origin and purpose.

And it is not difficult to ascertain wherein sovereignty,

thus conceived, resides. It is not in any government, whatever its form may be; nor yet in the individuals of any nation, however numerous they may be; but *in the State as a juristic person*, the organized community as a totality of interrelated personal possessors of rights.

Did sovereignty exist *before* the State? If it did, if it belonged to individuals separately out of a State-relation, each one must possess some small portion of it; and there would be in existence *greater* or *lesser* sovereignties, according to the size of the populations combining to form States. But sovereignty is not a material combination made up of parts. Like consciousness, which is not made up of bits of feeling but is an organic unity, sovereignty first comes into being through a coördination of parts that are already in organic relations. Men do not consent to form a State until they already form a society, and sovereignty makes its appearance for the first time when a society becomes conscious of its rights and of the necessity of regulating conduct by public law.

THE IMPORT OF LOCKE'S THEORY FOR INTERNATIONAL SOCIETY

Entirely preoccupied with the internal constitution of the State, Locke did not extend his theory to the broader form of society then just beginning to be realized; and no one appears, so far as we are aware, to have given it the attention it deserves in its application to the Law of Nations.

In seeking the foundations of the State in a "compact," and in pointing out that the substance of a compact is "consent," Locke prepared a basis for a far wider organization of human society than was contemplated in his "Treatise of Civil Government." If the State itself rests upon an agreement assented to by those who are subject to its laws, if the formula for authoritative law is "the consent of the governed," and if sovereignty is not supremacy to law but free self-determination within the limits of juristic relations, it would appear as if the society of States is quite as capable of jural organization as the members of any single community; for, thus regarded, the whole system of social organization is not something imposed from above by a superior power, but something developed from within by the free rational activity of man in response to his imperative social needs.

It may be true, that the society of States is as yet in "the state of nature," and that no adequate provision has yet been made for protecting the rights of States corresponding to that which is afforded by the State for the defence of the rights of individuals, and that each one must do as all men did before the State existed, fight its own battles and exact the power with which to do so; but is there any inherent impediment, except purely arbitrary and wrongful opposition, to the further development of this larger society along lines analogous to those followed by the smaller?

The powers of government, according to Locke, are in general properly directed toward providing remedies for the evils that existed in "the state of nature." These evils may be described, in Locke's language, as follows; and it is interesting to note how entirely the evils still existing in the society of States correspond to those enumerated as needing remedy before the State existed: —

"First, there wants an established, settled, known law, received and allowed by common consent to be the standard of right and wrong, and the common measure to decide all controversies between them: for though the Law of Nature be plain and intelligible to all rational creatures; yet men being biassed by their interest, as well as ignorant for want of study of it, are not apt to allow of it as a law binding upon them in the application of it to their particular cases.

"Secondly, in the state of nature there wants a known and indifferent judge, with authority to determine all differences according to the established law: for everyone in that state being both judge and executioner of the law of nature, men being partial to themselves, passion and revenge are very apt to carry them too far, and with too much heat in their own cases; as well as negligence, and unconcernedness, which make them too remiss in other men's.

"Thirdly, in the state of nature there often wants power to back and support the sentence when right, and to give it due execution. They who by any injustice offended will seldom fail, when they are able, by force to make good their injustice; such resistance many times makes the punishment dangerous, and frequently destructive, to those who attempt it."[1]

THE MANDATE OF MAN TO HIS GOVERNMENTS

These then are the three deficiencies in his original condition for which Man has supplied remedies through the State: (1) a clear statement of jural, as distinguished from moral, law; (2) an impartial interpretation and application of jural law; and (3) its effective enforcement. Is it impossible for similar deficiencies in the society of States to be provided for in a similar manner?

If the wrongs men endured and the losses they suffered in a "state of nature" drove them to seek refuge in the State as

[1] Locke, *Treatise on Civil Government*, Book II, Chap. IX.

an embodiment of law, is it probable that civilized nations, with this example before them, will consent to live forever in a state of perpetual war, or in frequent expectation of it, or in constant preparation for it?

The mandate of Man was issued, and the Modern State appeared. It is he who has evoked it from the shame of slavery and the despotism of unbridled power. Will he not in his own time speak again? Having created governments by the authority of his inherent rights, and having hedged them about with constitutions for his better security, having bidden them to make laws, equal and just for all men within the State, will he not command his governments to give to human rights a still stronger guarantee, by extending the reign of law between all nations, and by building upon foundations of impartial justice between States a permanent assurance of international peace?

V

THE STATE AS A SUBJECT OF POSITIVE LAW

HAVING seen that a society of States really exists, and that it is of a nature to be regulated by laws, we are now prepared to inquire, what laws are adapted to its needs, whether they already exist or may be brought into existence, and by what criterion their authority may be determined.

Before we proceed to pursue this inquiry, however, we may perhaps be aided by ascertaining what it is that is common to civilized nations, and what is the bond which unites Sovereign States in a society.

WHAT IS CIVILIZATION?

When we contemplate the complexity of modern social existence in what we call "civilized" countries, it seems at first difficult to state precisely what it is that constitutes "civilization." We can perhaps most easily separate what is essential to it from what is non-essential by considering the course of social development in the countries we call "civilized" as contrasted with that in countries we call "uncivilized."

When we compare the extremes thus brought into contrast, we observe in the countries that pass for "civilized" the presence of art, science, industry, — especially mechanical industry, — literature, and education; while, in those that pass for "uncivilized," we either note a total absence of these, or find them existing in a very rudimentary form. We might, therefore, not unnaturally infer, at first thought, that it is these forms of culture which together constitute civilization; but, upon a little reflection, we should perceive, that they are in truth only the outward signs of civilization. If we study them in their development, we become aware that they are the result of the manifold activities of a people actuated by a spirit of individual initiative expressing itself in a great variety of forms. Whence arises this general impulse to self-expression which characterizes the civilized community, in contrast to the general inertia and uniformity of type to be found among an uncivilized people?

All of these varied manifestations spring directly from the free exercise of human faculties, stimulated and favored by conditions conducive to their development. In order to apprehend the true nature of civilization in a causal sense, we must look beyond the mere phenomena, and try to discover the conditions which determine them.

Our first thought might be, that these conditions are to be sought in the physical environment, and the social needs and opportunities produced by it; but when we examine closely into the influence which nature alone exercises upon human activity, we learn that natural beauty does not invariably inspire art, that wealth of natural resources does not always induce industry, and that variety of natural production does not of itself promote commerce.

If we endeavor to seek these conditions in the nature of the individuals who exhibit the marks of civilization, and attribute their origin to the influence of race, we meet with even greater difficulties; for, historically, these forms of culture are shown to be, not attributes of race, but the outgrowth of social conditions. It may be that special aptitudes for art, science, industry, and so forth, are possessed by certain races and not by others; but these aptitudes have always remained merely latent, and have never come to fruition, until social conditions favorable to their exercise were provided.

We are, therefore, driven to the conclusion, that these outward signs, or manifestations, of civilization are the result of the free unfolding of human energies under social conditions favorable for their exercise; and we find these conditions in the protection afforded to person and property by the State; which sets free, and renders active, the multiform energies which, without this protection, remain dormant and unproductive, because there exists no certainty that effort will be rewarded. Under the conditions of a "state of nature," neither person nor property has any security. There is, therefore, no motive, and there is but little opportunity, for any form of activity, except that which is necessary for immediate personal needs. But, when released from the necessity of self-defence and the feeling of insecurity by the assurance that the person will be protected and the right of property respected, each member of the community is stimulated to the full exercise of his mental powers for the attainment of that form of good which he most desires. From the moment of that assurance, the latent aptitudes become active, and the outward signs of civilization spontaneously appear.

Although there may be a specific relation between different forms of culture and different forms of government, the essential condition of civilization is not to be found in any particular form of government; for it may flourish, to some extent at least, as history proves, under any form of government which approximately realizes the purpose of the State. The essential condition is, that this purpose be in some degree realized; since, without it, the free development of human faculties is hindered, and the flower of culture withers because it is impoverished at its roots.

THE STATE THE MEASURE OF CIVILIZATION

It is true, that history reveals the presence of some of the most conspicuous signs of civilization where the idea of the State has failed of a perfect, or even a very high, form of realization. Under the patronage of rich and powerful princes who have sapped the energies of the people for their private benefit, art and literature have flourished through their bounty; but industry, misdirected, overtaxed, and rendered timid and lacking in enterprise through their cupidity and exactions, has visibly languished. Commerce may thrive under a régime of monopoly, while the people suffer through oppression. Every form of State protection or neglect bears its natural fruit, whether it be of good or of evil; but the rule holds, that the character of civilization is determined by the extent to which the idea of the State is realized. The reason for this is inherent in the necessary relation of human faculties and powers of production to the degree of freedom and security with which they may be exercised.

If the foregoing exposition be correct, the standard of measurement by which the degree of civilization attained by a nation or community of men is determined, is to be found in the organization of the State. That standard is the extent to which the juristic idea is incorporated in its laws and policies.

This truth becomes more evident the farther we pursue the inquiry. It is not merely the external splendor of life, in any of its forms or manifestations, that constitutes civilization. Some of its external signs — such as art, industry, and certain forms of commerce taken in isolation — may exist through the patronage or compulsion of despotic power, even in a relatively barbaric country. The confirmation of the assertion that the State is the *fons et origo* of civilization is, however, found in the fact that these signs do not appear in any great number where the State has not preceded them; and in the further fact, that they never coexist in any symmetrical combination, except where a high realization of the purposes of the State has set free, and called into action, the human powers that produce them. We see, therefore, that the perfection of the State is the true measure of civilization, since the State is the determining principle from which civilization proceeds.

It is, therefore, not to the outward signs, — the arts, the sciences, literature, and commerce, — that we must look for the improvement of civilization, but to the primary cause. Neither skill, nor knowledge, nor expression, nor luxury can master and destroy barbarism; which some of these may, however, serve to decorate. That which puts upon a community the stamp of civilization is the security of rights under just laws; that is, the degree of effectiveness with which the juristic idea of the State is realized.

Measured by this standard, the civilization of a country does not depend upon its territorial extent, or the number of its inhabitants, or the wealth they may happen to possess. A country is civilized exactly in proportion to the degree in which it recognizes, applies, and respects those principles of justice which the State was instituted to enforce. Its soil may be poor, its cities few and small, its people plain and frugal; but if it maintains the rights of all to life, liberty, and the free exercise of their powers of self-development, with security for all against wrong, that is a civilized country in the best sense of the word. Unless civilization in this its proper sense is rooted in the convictions and supported by the determination of the people, it is wholly illusory to imagine that a nation is civilized.

THE ESSENTIAL UNITY OF CIVILIZATION

We perceive then that civilization, properly conceived, is not a mere casual collocation of outward manifestations, but a process of transformation in the life of mankind. It is the substitution of order for disorder, and of liberty for bondage. It is the progressive setting free of human energies for the accomplishment of higher and nobler tasks, in all the fields of human activity, by giving them a more complete security.

We cannot, therefore, speak of *different* civilizations. There is but *one* civilization. When we speak of the "civilizations of antiquity," — of Assyria, Egypt, and Greece, for example, — what we have in mind is not different "civilizations," but different forms of culture. When we, through the inexactness of our language, — so rich in most respects, — speak of the "history of civilization," meaning thereby the history of "culture," — which the Germans so well express by "Kulturgeschichte," — we mislead ourselves, and so come at last to think of civilization as a sum of outward manifestations, instead of an inner principle or process of evolution.

The Latin origin of the word should have preserved us from this error, which has probably grown out of the habit of contrasting civilization, as a complex of causes and effects, with "barbarism"; which is neither a cause nor an effect, but simply a condition of existence, or stage of human advancement, only a little higher than that of savagery.

But when we think of civilization as a process of development, ever tending toward one constant goal, namely, the amelioration of the condition of mankind through the free unfolding of human faculties under the protection of civic security, we comprehend, that, while there are various degrees of approach to the attainment of this end, there is and must be a perfect unity in the process itself; and that, therefore, all civilized States, although unequal in their approximation to the goal, are all, presumably, endeavoring to attain it.

If this assumption be well founded, we may expect to find among all civilized nations a gradual acceptance of the same principles, and a gradual unanimity in applying them; and this the history of the society of States teaches us has been the case.

As we have already seen, it was not until the time of Grotius that any general Law of Nations was recognized by any writer as being worthy of serious discussion; and Grotius found that law so meager, so uncertain, and so unsatisfactory to rational intelligence, that he thought it necessary to supplement and improve it through new deductions from the Law of Nature, as he understood that expression. We have seen also, that the first great apostle of the doctrine of Grotius, Pufendorf, found the Law of Nations so full of contradictions, that he did not esteem it to be law at all, in any proper jural sense; and, returning to the vague idea of a Law of Nature, undertook to deduce from it the rules that should govern States as "moral persons"; thus reducing the

Law of Nations to international morality, binding upon the conscience but not enforceable in fact.

Whatever may be said of the practices of States, it is worthy of note, that, from that time forward to the present day, in every civilized country of the world, international jurisprudence has been considered as a science worthy of the attention of the greatest minds; and many of the greatest minds have been devoted to it. Like every other branch of human knowledge, it has passed through many stages of development, and has been the object of different opinions; but the important fact is, that certain principles are now universally recognized, not only as morally binding, but as furnishing a basis for positive rights, unquestioned by any civilized government, and which every civilized government would consider it proper to enforce. The essential unity of civilization is, therefore, no longer a mere theory; it is an undisputed fact.

THE OPPOSITION OF "NATURALISTS" AND "POSITIVISTS"

It does not lie within the purpose of this discussion, to follow in detail either the historical development of the laws which have been recognized as authoritative for the society of States, or of the science that deals with those laws; but it is important that we should, in this connection, form a clear idea of the nature of the laws applicable to the conduct of civilized nations, the form in which they are supposed to exist, and the kind of authority upon which they are founded.

Without attempting to answer in an exhaustive manner any of the questions here suggested, it may be well to call attention, first, to the conflict of opinion between the "Naturalists," who have sought to build up a system of international jurisprudence based upon the "dictates of right reason," or the interpretation of the Law of Nature; and the "Positivists," who have rejected the applicability, and sometimes even the existence, of the so-called "Law of Nature," as being in no sense real law; and have contended, that there exists a body of positive rules, so clearly and generally recognized by all civilized governments, that they may be esteemed, in a substantial sense, as constituting the Law of Nations, to the exclusion of everything else.

At the beginning, the Naturalist school of thought had every advantage, and possessed the most weighty names. In Germany, Christian Thomasius (1655–1728); in England, Thomas Rutherford; in France, the learned Jean Barbeyrac (1674–1744); and in Switzerland, the famous Genevan, Jean Jacques Burlamaqui (1694–1748), were noted followers of the line of thought opened by Pufendorf. All these laid stress upon the Law of Nature as the great and authoritative source of the laws that should govern in the intercourse of States.

The honor of founding the Positivist school may properly be accorded to Richard Zouch (1590–1660), a contemporary of Grotius, and Professor of Civil Law at Oxford. In the title of his most important book, he used the expression *Jus inter Gentes*, or Law *between* Nations; instead of *Jus Gentium*, or Law *of* Nations, which Grotius employed; and thus in substance proposed the designation which Jeremy Bentham (1748–1832) applied to this branch of law, when he christened it "*Inter*national Law," — the name which has since come into most common use.

Although Zouch did not deny the existence of the Law of Nature, he paid little attention to it; considering that the only real, or positive, law is the law actually in effect; and this he found in the "customs" of nations.

Following upon these lines, the German jurists Samuel Rachel (1628–1691) and Johann Wolfgang Textor (1637–1701) considered the Law of Nations as consisting in the rules of action to which a plurality of free States are, by their express or tacit "consent," subjected. The Dutch jurist Cornelius van Bynkershoek (1673–1743) laid stress upon International Law as found in treaties between States. Johann Jakob Moser (1701–1785), a German professor, added great strength to this direction of thought by compiling a vast collection of facts, gathered from usage and treaties; and George Friedrich von Martens (1756–1821) rendered an immense service to it by his celebrated "Recueil des Traités," which has grown to be an enormous repository of state documents, of whose beginnings he made good use in his "Précis."

THE ADHERENTS OF GROTIUS

Although the so-called "Law of Nature" is at present regarded by the Positivist school as non-existent, — and that school tends at present perhaps to become the prevailing one, — the main line of development in the treatment of International Law has followed the general plan laid down by Grotius. The reason for this course of development is plain. During the centuries since Grotius wrote, as international experience has widened, an immensely increased number of international rules based on usage have been generally accepted; thus giving to positive law a vastly augmented range and consistency, as compared with what it had in the earlier period. But when we turn our attention to the manner in which this growth has proceeded, we are obliged to admit, that it is not the result of mere unconscious or unreasoned accretion, but of the steady application of the principles which were first supposed to be derived from the Law of Nature. Whatever may be now said of the vagueness or the non-existence of that alleged source of authority, it cannot be disputed, that, as a fact of history, the "dictates of right reason" — to use the formula of Grotius and his early followers — have had a large influence in determining the customs and the treaty provisions on which the Positivist school now triumphantly bases its claims to the existence of a positive Law of Nations. Nor can it be denied, that this growth would have been a meager one, if the Naturalists had not persistently pushed the claim of purely moral principles as binding upon the consciences of statesmen and diplomatists, and worthy to be followed in practice.

From this point of view, we are able to appreciate the fertility of the method which Grotius adopted; and, although the substance of his teaching now seems to us, in many respects, crude, narrow, and antiquated, his recognition on the one hand of existing usages, and on the other of principles by which those usages might be ameliorated, marks the clearness of his insight into the nature of the materials to which he was endeavoring to give the form of a science, and the breadth of his intelligence in embracing in his system the two different but essential coefficients of legal progress.

A confirmation of the view here presented is found in the fact that the Positivist school itself has never been able to dispense entirely with a resort to general principles wider than the positive laws it has found in existence, until, in the latter part of the nineteenth century, the application of those principles had produced a mass of positive results so great that

International Law seemed to have taken on the substance of an independent reality. But it appears doubtful if a resort to general principles is even now, or ever can be, wholly neglected by writers who may attempt to present even the positive law in a complete and systematic form. It is only in a qualified sense, that we may say, that there is any writer of the Positivist school who has covered the entire field of International Law in strict conformity with its theory. In every one of the books that might be mentioned, there are arguments from general principles as to what International Law really is; which is equivalent to saying, that every writer on the subject helps out his exposition with what he considers the "dictates of right reason" on the subject. Among modern writers, we are, therefore, compelled to conclude, the Positivists are those who endeavor to show what they think the positive Law of Nations is, rather than to indicate what they think it ought to become.

WOLF'S CONCEPTION OF A WORLD-STATE

Among the older writers who have left a deep impression on international jurisprudence, must be mentioned Christian Wolf (1679–1754), a professor of philosophy at Halle who exercised a predominating influence in the time between Leibnitz and Kant, but whose voluminous writings are at present almost forgotten.[1]

The chief contribution of Wolf to the science of jurisprudence is his clear discrimination between individual and political rights and obligations. States, he holds, like individual

---

[1] The most important for International Law are: *Jus Gentium Methodo Scientifico Pertractatum*, 1749; and *Institutiones Juris Naturae et Gentium*, 1750.

persons, have inherent rights; and are, therefore, bound by corresponding reciprocal duties. From this point of view, law is, by the nature of things, inherent in the society of States, in the same sense that it is embodied in the single States which compose that society.

We have here then a perfectly logical conception of the jural unity of all civilized States. We are not surprised, therefore, to find Wolf advocating a *Civitas Maxima*, or World-State, as the ideal unity of which all civilized States form coördinate parts. All are bound together, he says, as members of this higher system of rights and duties, as truly as individuals are bound together in the reciprocal relations of a single State. In the "World-State," "every nation owes to every other nation what it owes to itself, so far as the latter does not possess it, and the former can furnish it without neglect of its duty to itself."

This conception of a "World-State," not in the Roman sense of a universal empire, but in the sense of a higher community of free and independent commonwealths, cannot fairly be dismissed as a mere dream of a metaphysician. Granted that States do possess inherent rights, just as individual persons possess them, how is it possible to escape the conclusion, that the totality of such juristic persons forms a juristic community characterized by unity in respect to its coherence, and reciprocity in respect to its interrelations? Upon the conditions given, the existence of a "World-State," *in the juristic sense*, is as clear and as conclusive as any demonstration of geometry.

It is also evident that Wolf could never have intended to teach that such a "World-State" exists in any other than a juristic sense. No one can believe that, because a logical composition of mutual rights and obligations involves the conception of a "World-State" in an ideal sense, that such a State is to be regarded as an existing human institution.

It may, however, well be considered, that such a "World-State," being a logical correlate of the most necessary juristic conceptions, presents an ideal toward which, so far as practicable, it is rational for mankind to work. We may even go a step farther than this, and say, that, whatever may be the apparent obstacles to such a consummation, it is not inconceivable that this ideal may at some future time be realized. If, as we have maintained, civilization is essentially one, and is everywhere aiming at the universal recognition and security of all human rights, it would appear, that, in time, the natural and almost inevitable result of this process will be the creation of a positive juristic order in the world not widely different from the "World-State" as it was conceived by the philosopher of Halle.

THE RÔLE OF JURISPRUDENCE IN DIPLOMACY

The speculative character of Wolf's theory rendered his work of comparatively small practical value to those who wished to know what was actually accepted by statesmen as positive International Law. An immense service was, therefore, rendered by Emerich de Vattel (1714–1767), a Swiss diplomatist, who was also engaged in the official service of Saxony and Poland, in applying to the juristic doctrines of Wolf corrections derived from a long experience with the real world of diplomatic negotiation.

As might well be expected, Vattel found in Wolf's teaching a useful solid groundwork for diplomatic action; but of course could not accept the idea of a "World-State" as a positive institution, or as dictating the positive Law of Nations. Accepting the doctrine of Wolf regarding the inherent rights of States as philosophically sound, Vattel, however, undertook to apply it in the sphere of practice. It is the first work on International Law in which are combined a clear grasp of controlling principles and an ample practical knowledge of the facts, methods, and conditions of actual statesmanship as pursued at the time, distinctly marking out the common ground of the jurist and the diplomatist.

The result was not dissimilar to that of applying pure mathematics to the concrete problems of engineering; and it was seen that, just as abstract mathematical truth is applicable to natural phenomena, although there are in nature no perfect circles but only approximations, so the abstract rights of States, while theoretically convenient for structural purposes, cannot at once be fully embodied in any legal system.

Although remote from the field of actual practice, Wolf himself perceived that this impossibility existed, because "rights" of necessity are limited by the conditions of a community. If, for example, but one man existed in the world, he would have a right to the whole of it; but when a man is placed in a society of other men possessing equal "rights," it is evident that the "rights" of each individual are in effect modified and limited by the fact of his living in a community; and something like this is true of States.

Since the perfect realization of all abstract rights becomes practically impossible in a society, Wolf admitted that some rights, owing to this limitation, are "imperfect"; and cannot, therefore, be enforced. Other "rights," being capable of perfect realization, may and should be enforced; and here is the sphere of positive International Law.

Drawing upon his large experience as a diplomatist, Vattel

produced a work full of detailed knowledge and practical good sense, which has been, and still is, greatly prized by statesmen and diplomatists, because it was for a long time the most successful combination of the great principles of jurisprudence with an appreciation of the concrete conditions in which diplomacy has to act;[1] and it hardly requires to be stated, that diplomatic procedure has been, and will always continue to be, the chief creative agency in the development of positive International Law. However much and often it has been employed for selfish and perverted ends, the legitimate task of diplomacy is, progressively, as occasion offers, to incorporate just and sound juristic ideas into the practice of nations; for by this means, and by this means only, can usage be ameliorated, and the progress of civilization in international affairs be promoted.

It is, indeed, sometimes imagined that the function of a diplomatist is to secure the greatest amount of possible immediate advantage for his country, and that he may employ any means to secure that object, if he can only achieve success. But this is merely the crude inference of the novitiate, or of the unthinking and uninstructed observer. The authoritative tribunal in this matter is not the pleased populace that applauds a national victory in a trial of skill, even though won by deceit and unfair conduct; but history, which measures success and failure by a different standard, — that of lasting benefit. Charged with the high responsibility of guarding and promoting the real interests of his country in their largest sense, the diplomatist who is trained in the school of history does not doubt, that, in the end, the highest and most permanent interest of his people is best served by

[1] Vattel, *Le Droit des Gens, ou Principes de la Loi Naturelle Appliqués à la Conduite et aux Affaires des Nations et des Souverains*, 1758.

demanding nothing that is not just, and at the same time permitting no one to impose upon his country injustice without protest and resistance. The more diplomacy becomes intelligent, the more will it strive to apply juristic principles to the ever-growing Law of Nations; and it is, therefore, of high importance that the diplomatist should be, in some sense at least, a jurist also.

THE NATURE AND AUTHORITY OF INTERNATIONAL LAW

We should now be able to comprehend and appreciate what it is that gives to International Law such authority as it possesses. As we have seen, considered merely as "morality," it would have no authority whatever, except as it is felt to be binding upon the consciences of statesmen, which are too variable to give it any high degree of certainty.

There are writers who deny that there exists any law international in a strictly jural sense. Among them is the celebrated English jurist John Austin (1790–1859), who defines "law" as "the commands issued by a sovereign authority to persons in general subjection to it;" which, of course, excludes altogether Bentham's idea of a law *between* States, they having no political superior, or sovereign power, over them.

It is clear, however, that this conception of jural law is too narrow to apply even within a single State. Statute law, made by a congress, a legislature, or parliament, is, without doubt, as good law as any; but such laws are not "commands issued by a sovereign authority." They are, rather, *agreements* as to what shall be received as law, made by the persons set apart for the purpose of legislation. And so also are treaties, which make law between nations; which are by our

Constitution, when duly ratified, "the supreme law of the land."

In the English-speaking world, we have laws based upon "custom," and those made — or as others would say, "declared" — by the decisions of judges. If, however, rules of action based upon custom, or upon judicial decisions, be considered jural law in the proper sense, then without doubt International Law not only exists, but has, within its sphere, the same reality as municipal law.

If we ask, what, in the most general sense, is Law, as distinguished from Morality? perhaps the most satisfactory answer is: Law, in the jural sense, is that body of rules which by the general consent of the community to which it applies may be enforced by public action.

In determining what the law is, it is not necessary to find a rule that is *certain* to be enforced; for under the most perfect governments it is sometimes impossible to enforce the law. The grossest crimes may go unpunished, because the means of detection and the judicial remedies are thwarted or eluded. The law remains, notwithstanding these evasions, absolutely unaffected by them.

The one essential characteristic of a jural law is, that there exist a general consent to its enforcement. If the idea be not definitely expressed, the reason is to be found in the indefiniteness of the idea itself; for jural law is by its nature a matter of opinion. When we go to a lawyer to find out what the law is, he gives us his "opinion." When the judge has decided the case against him, it is by the authority of his "opinion"; which in turn may be reversed by the "opinion" of a higher court. What all agree may be enforced is undoubtedly the law, whether it is known through prevailing custom, explicit legislation, or the decision of a judge.

That International Law really exists, and is jurally as well as morally binding upon States, is explicitly recognized by all, and has been formally declared by most of them. By the declaration of Aix-la-Chapelle, of November 15, 1818, the sovereigns of Europe engaged "never to depart, either among themselves, nor in their relations with other States, from the most strict observance of the principles of the Law of Nations." In the declaration of Paris of April 16, 1856, the plenipotentiaries affirmed the existence of maritime law in time of war, and their intention to introduce fixed principles in this respect in international relations. The seventh article of the Treaty of Paris of March 30, 1856, admits the Sublime Porte to the advantages of "Public Law and of the European Concert"; and many other public declarations might be cited, to show that the existence and authority of a body of rules composing the substance of International Law are generally recognized by Sovereign States throughout the world.

We may rightly use the expression "throughout the world"; for, while International Law was at first regarded as existing for Christian nations only, then for European nations, and later for nations of European origin, it is now universally extended to all really autonomous and independent States; and all admit that they are subject to it. The Hague Conferences of 1899 and 1907 have officially placed the seal of equality upon all these Powers, without distinction, and confirmed their membership in the society of States. They have unanimously declared in solemn conventions their intention to establish by agreement "the principles of equity and right on which repose the security of States and the welfare of peoples."

THE PROPOSED CODIFICATION OF INTERNATIONAL LAW

It would, without doubt, add greatly to clearness in determining precisely what International Law in any specific case is, if it were formulated in an officially accepted code; but it has been erroneously urged, that International Law cannot really claim to be law until it is formally codified.

At a meeting of the British Association for the Promotion of Social Science, held at Manchester, in October, 1866, a motion was made by David Dudley Field for the appointment of a committee to prepare the outlines of an international code. The proposal was favorably regarded, and a committee of jurists of different nationalities was appointed; but the movement was not prosecuted to a conclusion. Mr. Field, however, bravely undertook to show what might be done; and, in 1872, published a volume covering the whole subject, which he had prepared unaided, under the title "Draft Outlines of an International Code." Previous to this, in 1868, Professor Bluntschli, of Heidelberg, had also published a work entitled "Modernes Völkerrecht der Civilisierten Staaten als Rechtsbuch Dargestellt," translated also into French under the title of "Droit International Codifié"; and in 1890 the Italian jurist Fiori published his "Il Diretto Internazionale Codificato." None of these publications has obtained official acceptance; but on October 10, 1873, at a conference of jurists held in Brussels, an association was established for the reform and codification of the Law of Nations, which in 1895 changed its name to "The International Law Association."

Although little of practical importance has resulted directly from these efforts, the founding of the "Institut de Droit International" at Ghent, in 1873, intended "to serve as an organ of the juridical opinion of the civilized world respecting International Law," has tended through its reports and discussions to clarify thought and promote a more perfect comprehension of possible lines for future development. The publication of several important reviews devoted to the same purpose has powerfully contributed to public enlightenment regarding the need of further progress in this direction.

But jurists, on the whole, have maintained much reserve on the desirability of codification. While the existence of a code would undoubtedly be a great convenience, it is felt by many that it would in effect arrest the organic growth of International Law, and stifle its life in imperfect formulas. Others fear that such an attempt to formulate international rules would open the way for including among them untried and merely academic maxims, which might either fail of practical acceptance, or, if accepted, prove embarrassing to the whole movement toward legalizing international relations. It has even been denied, that International Law, without codification, is more indefinite than municipal law often has been in countries which have attained a considerable degree of legal advancement. So high an authority as Professor Westlake, of Cambridge University, says: "Take, for instance, the laws of England in the period of Glanville and Bracton, say the reigns from Henry II to Henry III, when old local customs, new feudal principles and habits of action, and a good deal of Roman law, then lately made known in this country, were being fused together in our common law, and that by the judges, to whom but little express legislative help was given before Edward I. While the process was going on, uncertainty reigned over as large a part of the law of England as the part of International Law over which it now reigns. And if we add the private violence, which then exceeded in frequency and impunity the public violence of European States in the nineteenth century, it may safely be said that International Law is now not less certain and is better obeyed than was the law of England till the process referred to was fairly complete." [1]

England's law has never been codified, and yet has grown to be a lucid and definite system. "The King's court rapidly created a body of clear, consistent, and formulated law. The itinerant justice, as he went from county to county, carried with him this law of the entire nation. From these beginnings arose the Common Law, the product of as high an order of political genius as the Constitution itself, and now the law of wider areas and of more millions of men than ever obeyed the law of Rome." [2]

It was once thought that codes would have the practical effect of diminishing litigation; but it has been proved by experience that this is not the case. There always remains something for the court to decide with regard to the question, What is the law? and the French law reports show, that there are more decisions on points of law than in the English reports covering the same period. Still, if it could be agreed upon, a general code of International Law would furnish a useful basis of decision, and would at least meet the objection that this branch of law is not yet clear.

THE CONTEMPORARY EVOLUTION OF INTERNATIONAL LAW

While theorists have been debating regarding the form which International Law should take, the process of evolution

---

[1] Westlake, *Chapters on the Principles of International Law*, Cambridge, 1894, pp. 8, 9.
[2] Adams, *The History of England* (1066–1216), London, 1905, p. 325.

has been quietly going on in the official world, with results that are worthy of all praise. Special branches of the Law of Nations have in fact been codified under official sanction, and the practically universal conventions in which they are contained assure for the whole civilized world not only progress but uniformity as regards these branches. Take, for example, the definite codes adopted by the Hague Conferences, and ratified by nearly all the governments, regarding the opening of hostilities; the laws and customs of war on land; the rights and duties of neutral powers and persons in case of war on land; the status of enemy merchant ships at the outbreak of hostilities; the conversion of merchant ships into warships; the laying of automatic submarine contact mines; bombardment by naval forces in time of war; the adaptation to naval war of the principles of the Geneva Convention; and the rights and duties of neutral powers in naval war. To these may be added the declaration regarding maritime warfare adopted by the Conference of London in 1909.

It is true, that the conventions named deal chiefly with rules that relate to war; but it signifies much, that it has been found possible to regulate armed conflicts by legal principles of a definite character, and this affords a promising prospect that eventually all other phases of international relations will be officially studied in detail and reduced to a concrete form of expression.

We are not perhaps sufficiently appreciative of the unostentatious but immediately fruitful application of rules to a host of international relations which touch our daily lives in time of peace, and which have been put into successful operation by common agreement. Nothing could better illustrate the essential unity of civilization than the unanimity with which the international enterprises now referred to have been brought into existence. As examples, take the Universal Postal Union, established by thirty States in 1878, after the successful experiment by twenty-one States begun four years earlier, and now augmented to sixty members, covering practically the whole civilized world, with congresses every five years, and a permanent central office at Berne; the Universal Telegraphic Union, established in 1868, comprising thirty States, also with a permanent central office; the Union for Railway Transportation, established in 1890, of which the chief European States are members; the Union for the Protection of Industrial Property, established in 1883; that for the Protection of Works of Literature and Art, formed in 1886; the Union for the Publication of Customs Tariffs, 1890; and the effort for the establishment of general rules regarding the conflict of laws, or Private International Law. To these should be added the conventions for common action regarding sanitary matters, weights and measures, monetary affairs, the preservation of wild animals, the extinction of the diseases of plants, and other subjects of general interest.

THE SUBJECTION OF THE STATE TO THE REIGN OF LAW

When we enumerate these triumphs of international intercourse, it may appear for a moment as if Wolf's conception of a "World-State" is already so far on the road to fulfilment that we cannot doubt its ultimate consummation; and that no real problems of world organization, except in matters of detail, remain for solution. But it would be unwise to deceive ourselves in this respect. In the matters we have just enumerated, there are no questions of conflicting rights or of opposing interests. Our common humanity has cried out in protest against the cruelties and barbarities of war, as it was formerly conducted; and it has been seen that it is a common advantage to mollify the sufferings and diminish the injustice which the formerly customary practices of warfare entailed. The dignity of the State, as well as human sympathy, has rendered this necessary. A similar community of interests has dictated the formation of the various unions which have been named, as contributing to the general convenience of mankind in an age of world-wide intercourse.

But there is another aspect to international interests. There are economic and political advantages to be guarded, and perhaps to be acquired, which produce a divergence, and even a direct conflict, of what are esteemed to be rights and interests. In this realm of relations and activities a common interest does not always appear to predominate; and, therefore, to inspire mutual confidence and coöperation. It is difficult to carry prescriptive or conventional laws into this region of conflicting public rights and interests, and it is only by a close analysis of the elements entering into them that we can hope for the ultimate triumph of intelligence in perceiving that even here, and everywhere, the ultimate interests of civilized peoples are in truth identical.

What we may perhaps claim to have gained from the exposition already given is, the assurance that jural law, — composed of universal rules that ought to be enforced between nations, — not only exists, but is recognized by all, is at times appealed to by all, and would be made generally effective, if the means of doing so were present in the same sense that they are within the well-organized single State.

And perhaps one other consequence results from the course of thought that has thus far been followed, namely, that there is no intrinsic obstacle to be found in the nature of the Modern State, as it actually exists to-day, to its frank and complete

THE STATE AS A SUBJECT OF POSITIVE LAW 129

submission to International Law. It is no diminution or impairment of "sovereignty," in any sense that may be fairly ascribed to it, for a State, even the greatest and the most powerful in the world, to formulate with others just rules of action, to which it voluntarily agrees to give the force and effect of law; or to pledge itself, as the embodiment of law, to respect and obey those rules in its own conduct. It can, in truth, in no way better justify its own righteous claim to the confidence and obedience of its own subjects or citizens. "Nothing can secure for human government, and for the authority of law which it represents, so deep a respect and so firm a loyalty as the spectacle of sovereign and independent States, whose duty it is to prescribe the rules of justice and impose penalties upon the lawless, bowing with reverence before the august supremacy of those principles of right which give to law its eternal foundation." [1]

[1] Instruction to the Delegation of the United States to the First Hague Conference.

VI

THE STATE AS A MEDIATOR OF GUARANTEES

GRANTING the existence of a body of positive International Law which civilized nations generally regard as binding upon them, and which they agree ought, if possible, to be enforced; what is to happen, if, for reasons of its own, a particular government refuses to comply with its requirements?

Unless some other arrangements are made than those which now exist, it is evident, that a State, suffering injury through the violation of International Law, has no other means of redress than an appeal to armed force; and, if, as frequently happens, the injured State be weaker than the aggressor, there is no means of enforcing the law, and the wrong has to be endured.

Under these conditions, the society of States, composed of members having for their aim the enforcement of just laws, presents the anomaly of a system of relations in which law and justice have no organized security.

In order to protect themselves from violent aggression, and to secure the advantages of peace and just treatment by their neighbors, Sovereign States, having no superior to whom they could appeal for protection, have been accustomed to unite for their common defence by treaties of alliance. These have sometimes, and very frequently, been of a character to excite general alarm; for they have at times created combinations of force so powerful as to constitute a standing menace to others excluded from them. In earlier times, it was common for such combinations to be formed for offensive as well as defensive purposes; and in such cases, — rendered the more alarming by real or imaginary "secret clauses" in the treaties of alliance, — counter combinations were made necessary; thus creating a situation fraught with danger, and promoting the "fear and distrust" which have long characterized international relations.

THE GUARANTEES OF INTERNATIONAL EQUILIBRIUM

When such compacts became customary, it was soon perceived that a certain degree of safety might be obtained by balancing these combinations against each other in such a manner as to maintain what was known as "European equilibrium";[1] an idea now expanded into what might be called "international equilibrium," since extra-European powers of importance have come into being. This is the most ancient, but has proved to be a very imperfect form of guarantee, either of peace or of justice; and has been a prolific cause of international disturbance, partly because this equilibrium has been extremely unstable, but chiefly for the reason that it is founded on the idea of hostility, and not upon the idea of concord, as expressing the normal order of things. The assumption underlying it is, that the society of nations as a whole cannot by general agreement exist upon terms of peace and jus-

[1] The benefits arising from efforts to maintain equilibrium are stated by Donnadieu, *Essai sur la Théorie de l'Equilibre*, Paris, 1900; and Dupuis, *Le Principe de l'Equilibre et le Concert Européen*, Paris, 1909. The influence of the idea on International Law is discussed by Kaeber, *Die Idee des Europäischen Gleichgewichts*, Berlin, 1907, pp. 143, 153; who concludes "dass sie gerade das erreiche, was sie vermeiden wolle, ewigen Krieg und Blutvergiessen."

tice, and that security can be obtained only by balancing one group of States against another in such a manner as to check the power of one group by the power of the other. In the perfection of this physical balance of forces, upon this theory, lies the sole effective guarantee that peace will prevail, and that international justice will not be constantly violated.

It would display a singular ignorance of history, to deny that this principle of equilibrium, in spite of its frequent failures and the impulse it has given to the increase of armed force, has produced some useful results. For the Italian city-states, by which in modern times it was first practiced, it was perhaps the only effective guarantee of existence; for their animosities were bitter, violent, and perpetual. When Europe was threatened with the domination of imperialism, there was no other safety for the smaller States than combination, first against the House of Austria, and then against the House of Bourbon; and the principles of balance passed into the traditions of European statesmanship. Holland saved its existence by an appeal to it, and England from the time of Cardinal Wolsey has profited by a deadlock of the continental powers to build up her oversea empire.

It may be true, that, at the present time, the "Triple Alliance" is, theoretically at least, balanced by the "Dual Alliance," and that the smaller States feel it to be an advantage to be able, in case of need, to appeal from one to the other. But the transitory nature of political alliances, the fears that they may fail at some critical juncture, the efforts to keep them alive and to strengthen them, the counter efforts to undermine and destroy them, and their sudden transformations and collapses, while they make interesting chapters of diplomatic history, cause very anxious hours to those who depend upon them for their safety.

INADEQUACY OF THE SYSTEM OF EQUILIBRIUM

It is clear, that in two important respects the system of the balance of power falls far below the needs of the Modern State, especially of the State which is conscious of its juristic character.

First, it is a purely mechanical conception. Its value lies not in any moral quality but in the resultant sum of effective forces. So long as this system prevails, the augmentation of forces is the main thing to receive attention. It means ever increased armaments, because its value lies in the weight of armaments, and it becomes useless without them; and this is frankly confessed by its advocates. Thus, in his recent book on British international politics, M. Lémonon, after weighing very carefully the forces favorable and unfavorable to France, while appreciating the value of an *entente* with England, says: "Before an Anglo-French alliance could be concluded, it would be necessary that England should re-make its land army, and that it should be sufficiently strong to be of use and efficiency in France." [1] If this were the case, he adds, there would be no objection to a written alliance with England.

Second, the system of balance bases friendship mainly on the common fear of hostility. This is a weak support, for two reasons: it makes it the interest of the weaker of the allies to cultivate this fear of hostility, or even the hostility itself, because this is the chief ground of their association; and it is constantly exposed to being undermined by the other side through the creation of suspicion between the allies and by secret inducements to abandon the alliance. The history of Europe shows how kaleidoscopic have been the

---

[1] Lémonon, *L'Europe et la Politique Britannique*, Paris, 1910, pp. 529, 530.

mutuations of the groups which have been formed, often at great sacrifice, to maintain equilibrium.

It is evident upon close analysis, that the effort to balance forces is in no sense a guarantee of justice, either as between the balanced masses as a whole or between the parts of which they are composed. There has never been any assurance that, if brought into conflict, these masses could accept on either side any principle of justice as the standard of their action. They have, both in theory and in practice, relied entirely upon their calculations of sufficiency, and sought on each side to render it preponderant. On the other hand, as a corollary of the idea of balance, there has grown up the pernicious doctrine of "compensations." When one side of the balance has appeared to have acquired new strength, the other has often claimed the right to compensate itself for this advantage of its adversary by seizing neutral territory. As, in order to maintain equilibrium, acquisitions ought to be equal, every new increment of force on either side has seemed to warrant a corresponding increase on the other; and usually at the expense of innocent and helpless peoples. That this procedure might be supplied with some appearance of equity, the fertility of the soil, the amount of the population, and the strategic value of a new acquisition of territory have been taken into account; thus indefinitely complicating the problem of a just balance, and opening the way for unlimited counter claims under the cover of necessity. Thus every principle of justice has been repeatedly disregarded, until in the name of a system absolutely mechanical and based entirely on force, all natural limits have been disregarded, nationalities dismembered, whole nations effaced from the map, and distant continents partitioned by ruthless expropriation or compliant transaction.

It would not be just to cast reflections upon any particular nation for these results without an exact examination of the conditions that have occasioned them, and this lies outside the present purpose. It is, however, clear, that the system, necessary as it may have seemed at definite points in the course of its development, certainly does not express the juristic character of the State, and is not to be commended as a guarantee of international justice, which it so plainly disregards.

THE PRINCIPLE OF FEDERATION

Analogous to it in some superficial aspects, but far removed from it in spirit and purpose, is the principle of federation. The resemblances between the two systems are, however, only upon the surface. Both are endeavors to promote security by association and by the creation of a powerful resisting body, which may by its increased force ward off attacks from without, and thus secure peace and safety to its component parts; but here the similarity abruptly ends.

While equilibrium is based upon the assumption of hostility, federation rests on the assumption of amity. The former is primarily a device to render one's foes powerless to injure, and this result sets the limit to the compact. The latter recognizes a deeper and more far-reaching community of interests, and extends the juristic functions of the State by widening their scope of application. The one is negative and passive in its purposes, the other is constructive and active.

The first great example of the benefits of federation in modern times is the American Union. If the original thirteen colonies had clung tenaciously to their local sovereignty, which was not surrendered without hesitation, there would have resulted a condition in which conflicting interests would have led to recurrent wars or to expedients of alliance with one another, and probably also with foreign powers, to prevent them. Had the disruption of the Union been effected by the success of the Southern Confederacy, it is certain that foreign powers would have been drawn into the rivalry of the North and the South for predominance, and both would have been ultimately controlled by foreign influences. How different and how far less fortunate the position of all the States composing the Union would have been, it is not difficult to imagine.

In truth, soon after the war of independence, in what has been called the "critical period," the prospect of a united nation was esteemed by observers very slight. "The Americans," said an English writer of that time, "can never be united into one compact empire under any species of government whatever; a disunited people until the end of time, suspicious and distrustful of each other, they will be divided and subdivided into little commonwealths or principalities, according to natural boundaries, by great bays of the seas and by vast rivers, lakes, and ridges of mountains."

The second great example of federation is the present German Empire. From the time of the Middle Ages, Germany like Italy had been little more than a geographical expression, and the parts which now compose the German Empire had existed in almost constant hostility to one another. From the end of the predominance of the House of Austria at the Peace of Westphalia, some three hundred Sovereign Powers, large and small, existed in more or less restrained jealousy and enmity, most of the time under the alleged "protection" of foreign alliances, until Napoleon I greatly reduced them by absorption and amalgamation, and united many of them under his protectorate in the Confederation of the Rhine. The efforts to unify North Germany by federation, under the leadership of Prussia, finally resulted in the establishment of the present Empire, in which the States of South Germany eventually found a place.

In a different form, Italy also exemplified in its unification the great advantages afforded by political consolidation and the substitution of constitutional guarantees, embracing a wide area of previously conflicting powers, for the unstable equilibrium which was the only approach to security they had been able to attain.

Whether in the form of federation or consolidation, the extension of the powers of the State as a juristic entity has marked the entire growth of civilization. In feudal times, travel was impossible without an armed escort. It was the increase of royal power that divested the king's highways of bandits and robbers. It was the royal courts that redressed the wrongs inflicted by petty local despots. It was the rise of national navies that cleared the seas of pirates. But these triumphs are small compared with those of modern constitutional States, that is, States founded upon guarantees, by which absolutism as well as anarchy has been held in check.

When we consider what the federative principle has done for the United States and Germany by extending juristic relations to these vast aggregates of population, each living under one system of laws and entitled to submit their rights to the judgment of a federal court, it might appear that here is the true image of what the whole world ought to become. It might even appear to be the ultimate goal of human effort in the endeavor to perfect political organization and realize the universal triumph of the juristic conception of the State.

IMPEDIMENTS TO GENERAL FEDERATION

There are, however, many conditions which render remote, and perhaps for ever impossible, the complete federation of the world. The inequalities of political development and aptitude among the different nations and tribes of men, some of which are still without any form of juristic organization and apparently incapable of developing or applying it, render such an equal yoking of all portions of mankind impossible. Even among the recognized members of the society of nations who would have to be considered in any general association there are idiosyncracies and antipathies of tradition, condition, and purpose which are plainly incompatible.

But, aside from these impediments to a general or even more extensive application of the principle of federation than has yet been made, there are considerations of great importance which cannot be overlooked. National independence is often necessary to the preservation and development of ideals which are not only dear to the people who are devoted to them but precious to civilization as a whole. The deliquescence of certain populations which stand for valuable types of culture in the general mass of an artificially extended nationality would involve the surrender of much that is too useful to be lost. There can be no intermixture of various degrees of culture without a levelling down as well as a levelling up; and this is particularly true, where, in a federated nation, the moral, religious, and social standards must be adapted to a new general average of opinion, and made to conform to uniform laws. It cannot be expected, therefore, that small States attaching great importance to their right of determining their own destiny will readily permit themselves to be absorbed by larger States, through their preponderant influence upon

THE STATE AS A MEDIATOR OF GUARANTEES 139

customs, tendencies, and legislation. They may rightly consider, that independence is necessary to the manifold development of thought and character by which the world is so greatly enriched. Without doubt, the total obliteration of nationality would involve immense losses to mankind. Loyalty to ideals, beliefs, and traditions is as important to political communities as to individuals. It is in and through them that history finds its impulse to progress, and it is their development which gives it unity. The continuity of our relations to the past is quite as important as any relation which binds us to the present. Neither men nor communities can reasonably be expected to disregard those bonds which give the highest sanctity to life, or to efface those memories which are the source of its noblest inspirations.

THE LIMITATIONS OF INDEPENDENCE

There is often, no doubt, in the tenacious adherence to independence a large element of sentiment. While sentiment may and should be respected, on the ground that it may sometimes be a useful factor of progress, it must be admitted to be a very unsubstantial and unsafe foundation on which to build a political community. The desire for independence sometimes exists where it has no right to fulfilment, because it would lead to the formation of nominally sovereign powers incapable of bearing the responsibility and discharging the duties of a civilized State.

It is not reasonable to maintain that every group of human beings that wishes to form a separate political community has the inherent right to do so. In the latter part of the eighteenth and the early part of the nineteenth centuries, sympathy with the aspiration for independence was very strong;

for the reason that many peoples, possessing a distinctive character and fully capable of self-regulation, were suffering under an oppressive rule imposed upon them by arbitrary force. But it has become evident from experience, that independence without qualifications for self-government is not only not a benefit to those who possess it, but that it exposes the whole system of rights to danger when power is assumed by incompetent and irresponsible governments. It is easy to say that each people is at liberty to choose its own government, and that its degree of competency and responsibility is its own private affair; but such a dogma overlooks the rights of neighboring peoples and of the society of States as a whole, whose peace is often endangered by the persistent or recurrent anarchy of States not founded upon juristic principles, or not conducted in harmony with them.

Over against the sentimental grounds for independence may be set the practical fact of interdependence between existing political communities. The moment these enter into jural relations with one another, there is developed a great body of mutual rights and obligations which must be safeguarded. Civilized nations cannot permit barbarities to be perpetrated by their next door neighbors, any more than individuals living in a community can tolerate lawlessness on the part of other persons. Hence arise the rights of supervision, intervention, and compulsory reform; rights which, upon close analysis, are found to be rather of the nature of public duties.

INTERNATIONAL INTERVENTION AND SUPERVISION

It was in pursuance of this line of obligation, that the so-called "Concert of Europe" was formed, a syndicate of the

Great Powers acting — nominally at least — for the purpose of enforcing order in less perfectly organized and less highly developed States, whose conduct had become intolerable; but, unfortunately, this concert was so frequently actuated in its operations by conflicting national interests as to defeat in great measure the reforms which it professed to be aiming to accomplish. More recently, the United States, in the interest of tranquillity and humanity, without in the least wishing to extend its territories, — but not always fully understood by others as respects its philanthropic motives, — has twice occupied and attempted to regenerate Cuba, and is at present undertaking to maintain order in the Philippines.

It cannot be doubted that these supervisory undertakings are, to a certain extent, guarantees that juristic principles will be applied in portions of the world not yet completely brought under the rule of justice as opposed to the rule of force. In so far as they are loyal to the high sense of duty which justifies them, they are to be commended; and should be recognized as among the tasks which fall to the elder brothers in the family of mankind. But it is important that here also international guarantees should be given. As an evidence of high and unselfish purpose, the best form of guarantee is the open door of trade, the equality of rights for all nations in the domain of business enterprise, each protecting State taking only so much revenue from the inhabitants as may be necessary for the support of its administration. By this method, all the outlying portions of the world which might otherwise become the field of conflicting national interests, and even of armed strife, may be taken out of the arena of dispute, and placed under a just and educative police surveillance useful to their inhabitants and beneficial to all mankind.

THE PRINCIPLE OF NEUTRALIZATION

Independent States, which have proved their capacity to maintain a responsible government, being members of the society of States, possess equally perfect rights, without regard to the size of their territory or the extent of their population. Some of them may, however, from a material point of view, require special guarantees of rights which unaided they might not be able to defend against foreign aggression. This necessity has been in some cases recognized, and provided for by "neutralization"; that is, certain States have been declared "neutral" in the conflicts that may arise between their more powerful neighbors, and their independence has by special compacts been taken under the united protection of the guarantors.

Thus, Switzerland since 1815, Belgium since 1831, and Luxemburg since 1867 — while retaining their entire political independence, which is guaranteed by the Greater Powers — are by treaty rendered perpetually neutral. While this arrangement prevents making their territories the scene of hostilities, it does not deprive these States of the right of self-defence. On the contrary, it imposes upon them the duty of defending their neutrality to the best of their ability; but, as they enjoy the guarantee of the Powers that they will aid them in this respect, it is improbable that their neutrality will ever be violated. During the entire period since the neutralization of the three countries just named, their right of neutrality has been uniformly respected.[1]

By the neutralization of these countries, the Powers which border upon them have voluntarily renounced an apparent advantage in case of war; for, if this restriction did not exist,

[1] For the neutralization treaties, with comments, see Wicker, *Neutralization*, London and New York, 1911.

THE STATE AS A MEDIATOR OF GUARANTEES

the border State that could soonest mobilize its forces and take possession of the adjacent territory could thereby cover its own frontiers from attack, and thus obtain a considerable strategic advantage. It is evident, however, that, if defence is the object in question, it is greatly promoted by the erection of such moral barriers; for neutralization not only limits the field of hostilities but diminishes the avenues through which invasion is legally possible. There can be no doubt, that, in every instance where neutralization has been applied, the arrangement has been a wise and useful one for all the Powers concerned.

The extent to which the principle of neutralization might be properly carried out is, however, open to discussion. It may at first appear that it is capable of very extensive application, and that through general neutralization war might be prevented altogether, by reducing the great military States to mere enclaves, surrounded by neutralized territories, so that they could not attack one another.

It must, however, be remembered, that no neutralization can be effective without the guarantee of the principal military Powers; and that these would never consent to being so hemmed in with moral barriers that they could not act in case of necessity.

It is, therefore, chiefly to certain small States, not able to exercise any great degree of influence upon international policies in general, and to territories liable to be brought into the sphere of rivalry for colonial expansion, that the principle of neutralization may be most advantageously applied. It would appear to be specially adapted to the commonwealths which may, in the future, be formed under the educative influence of their present protectors, when they have become capable of self-government and no longer require to be treated as dependencies, yet may not be capable of self-protection without a degree of aid which it might not be expedient for any one Power alone to continue.

But the more crucial question is, what guarantees may be given, with regard to the security of their respective rights, by and to the greater national States? These are, indeed, able to protect themselves, and by their own force to see that their rights are respected; but, so long as this respect has no other support than armed force, it is highly improbable that it will be practicable to prevent armed conflicts between them; and it is certain that such trials of strength, being determined by force alone, and not by any principle of justice, can never be quite satisfactory to the jural consciousness of civilized States.

THE JURAL RELATIONS OF INDEPENDENT STATES

If, therefore, there is to be a world organization based on juristic conceptions, the Great Powers also must provide for a clear determination of their rights and a means of securing them without an appeal to force.

The proposal that mutual guarantees for this purpose, based on clearly defined principles, be exchanged, is by no means a novelty. When the efforts of the coalition of the Great Powers to suppress the imperial ambitions of Napoleon I had been crowned with success by his overthrow, it was considered of the highest importance to guard against a recurrence of the danger to which the peace of Europe had been exposed. To this end, the Congress of Vienna — which lasted from November 1, 1814, to June 9, 1815 — undertook to make a territorial settlement, which, it was hoped, might secure the future stability of international relations. Unfortunately, neither the principle of nationality nor the rights of peoples were considered in this adjustment, and new safeguards against revolution had to be devised. The religious temperament of the Emperor of Russia, Alexander I, influenced by the evangelical mysticism of Madame de Krüdener, led him to propose the "Holy Alliance," of September 26, 1815, by which it was intended that the armed strength of Europe should be united in the task of maintaining peace on the basis of the precepts of the Christian religion.

Noble as the intention of this compact may have been, it was impossible for Europe, at a time when nations were conscious that their rights were disregarded, to contemplate with equanimity the control of their destinies by a small group of monarchs united for the support of reactionary policies. The Holy Alliance would have failed entirely, had it not been supplemented by a renewal of the more specific obligations of the Treaty of Chaumont (March 1, 1814), which had served to unite Great Britain, Austria, Russia, and Prussia in their opposition to Napoleon. It was agreed that the Powers should "renew their meetings at fixed periods," and unite "to provide for the prosperity and repose of nations, and the maintenance of the peace of Europe" (November 20, 1815).[1]

But this compact made no provision for harmonious action in dealing with the constitutional aspirations of the peoples who were determined to enjoy the advantages of law and liberty afforded by the Modern State. It was presently perceived, on the other hand, that the weight of the coalition was intended to be placed in opposition to the constitutional movement, and to be employed as a deadly instrument of

---

[1] The treaties here referred to may be found in Martens, *Nouveau Recueil;* and Ouroussow, *Résumé Historique des Principaux Traités de Paix*, Evreux, 1884.

reactionary compulsion. It could not, therefore, be maintained; and the syndicate of Great Powers associated under it, in spite of the masterly activity of Metternich in attempting to dictate the policy of the allies, was unable to repress the rising tide of constitutionalism.

The efforts to preserve the peace of Europe by the united action of the Great Powers, therefore, ended in failure; not, however, because united action is intrinsically impossible, but because it was then applied for the purpose of arresting the irresistible progress of the Modern State in the process of self-realization. It cannot, therefore, be fairly inferred, that united action in aiding the process of normal development would meet with insurmountable obstacles. The Holy Alliance was engaged in the unholy task of suppressing jural development by the use of armed power. It would be a quite different enterprise, if Modern States should decide, by the aid of mutual guarantees, to establish more firmly the jural relations which they all recognize and affirm; and thereby substitute the security of law for the hazards and menaces of physical force.

THE ADAPTABILITY OF THE MODERN STATE FOR JURAL GUARANTEES

It is not inconsistent with the nature and character of the Modern State that it should give guarantees for its own conduct, since it is, in fact, founded upon them. In this it differs from the State in the time when absolutism was considered as marking its essential character. The struggles for constitutionalism have settled the right of the people to make their governments responsible to them, and the victory of this principle is now practically universal. It is no longer considered beneath the dignity of a government to serve under the restraints of constitutional guarantees; and these are now demanded, and in principle granted, in every civilized community.

Even the greatest and most powerful of modern rulers — by whatever names they may be designated — recognize the fact, that the State is an embodiment of law; and that their place in it is prescribed and secured by law. And thus, whatever the form of government may be, it possesses a legal guarantee upon which its right to exist depends.

Such guarantees within the State consist in the recognition of certain primary rights as inherent in its constituents, and in a division of powers so defined and limited as to secure to each one of them the benefits of justice before the law. These guarantees lose nothing of their value and efficiency from the fact that they have been voluntarily accorded; and it follows from the character of the Modern State that they may not justly be withheld.

It is evident, therefore, that the Modern State is peculiarly adapted to enter into juristic relations based on mutual guarantees with other States of like character. But international guarantees, with which we are here particularly concerned, have a place even more important to the welfare of nations than those which limit political powers within the State; for the reason, that the existence of the State, which without them is exposed to the contingencies of invasion and conquest, may depend upon their sufficiency. In some form, as we have seen, international guarantees have been found necessary by every form of government; and, in a rude way, they were sought and provided for long before modern constitutions were formed, or even dreamed of by the people of any modern country. It cannot, therefore, be regarded as a presumptuous encroachment upon the autonomy and independence of the State, if it be proposed, that these guarantees assume a form more in harmony with the juristic character of the present age.

If it be true, as all civilized governments profess, that no one of them would consider itself justified in embarking upon a scheme of public plunder; if the vast military and naval armaments of the present time are not intended for aggressive but solely for defensive purposes; then it would seem quite possible for Modern States, or for those of their number of whom this may be believed, to enter into such compacts as would largely if not entirely eliminate the probability of warlike collisions between them.

THE LIMIT AND BASIS OF INTERNATIONAL GUARANTEES

It may be said, and with perfect truth, that no government possesses the right to efface the State, to surrender its inherent rights, or to imperil its existence by the sacrifice of its essential prerogatives. It may not then give to any other State, or to any superior above the State, guarantees which involve its own immolation or loss of independence. This, however, is precisely what was proposed by the Holy Alliance. That document provides, that "the only binding principle, either between the said governments or their subjects, shall be that of rendering mutual service; of testifying to one another, by an unchangeable benevolence, the mutual affection by which they ought to be animated; of considering themselves only as members of the same Christian nation: the three princes regard themselves as merely the delegates of Providence, to govern three branches of the same family, thus confessing that the Christian nation, of which they and

THE STATE AS A MEDIATOR OF GUARANTEES 149

their peoples form part, has really no other sovereign than Him to whom belongs all power, because in Him alone are found the treasures of love, knowledge, and infinite wisdom, that is to say, God, our Divine Saviour Jesus Christ, the Word of the Most High, the Word of Life."

Beautiful as this effusion of feeling sounds, it does not propose any substantial guarantee of either peace or justice. It is rather the substitution of government by emotion in place of government by law; on condition, however, that three great armies, whose unity of action is otherwise provided for, shall sustain the decisions of this triple delegation of Providence regarding what brotherly love demands!

If statesmen could ever sanction such a wholesale effacement of national sovereignty as this famous treaty prescribes, it is difficult to see with what consistency they could object to the State's being bound by its own laws, — that is, laws whose jural validity and authority it voluntarily recognizes; and that is all that is still required in order to afford guarantees of justice between Sovereign States.

But it would be a feeble argument for international guarantees, to base their claims to a legal character on the precedent of an inoperant treaty which no jurist could defend; and the *argumentum ad hominem* would have no force, even for the States which were once briefly bound by that compact.

The solid ground for the justification of international guarantees based on juristic conceptions is found in the essentially juristic character of the Modern State. An argument against the utility of such guarantees would be a repudiation of the idea of the Modern State, as the embodiment of law, at a time when it is celebrating its final triumphs. Every modern nation aspires to the enjoyment of constitutional guarantees. In the last quinquennium, Russia, Persia, Turkey, and now

China have all felt the thrill of an awakening jural consciousness; and all have obtained, or are demanding, the guarantees of a legal constitution. And it is difficult to see, how this general movement, following upon the lines of development throughout the world, can logically terminate in a refusal to recognize in international affairs the principles it has evoked and applied in national affairs. Never before in the history of mankind has it been so clearly perceived as at the present moment, that the whole of civilization is based upon the existence of guarantees that force shall not prevail until the voice of justice has been heard. In what form justice is to be invoked, and in what manner its decisions are to be executed, may still be problematical; but the fact that these questions are pressing themselves with unexampled insistence upon public attention is the sufficient proof, that the jural consciousness of all civilized nations is demanding the discovery of some method by which the voice of justice may be heard in the intercourse of nations.

VII

THE STATE AS AN ARMED POWER

"The end of justice is peace, the means for attaining it is conflict. So long as justice is attacked by injustice, . . . so long will justice not be exempt from conflict. . . . All the justice in the world has been obtained by struggle; every important rule of right has had to be wrung from those who have opposed it; and every right, that of a people as well as that of an individual, presupposes the constant state of preparation to assert it." [1]

These are the words with which Rudolf von Ihering begins his famous book, — published in German in 1872, and translated twenty-one times into foreign languages, — "Der Kampf ums Recht."

Warlike as the title sounds, and overstrained as the argument may sometimes seem, the thesis, that "justice is not a mere thought but a living power," is a statement of unquestionable historical verity. It requires no elaborate reasoning to prove that Right has never possessed a firm foothold anywhere upon the earth until it has fought its battle with Wrong, either in the field or in the forum, and shown itself the stronger.

It is of no avail, therefore, to cry, "Peace, peace," where there is no justice, and no power to command it; for peace

[1] Ihering, *Der Kampf ums Recht*, Vienna, 1906.

without justice is ignominious, and wherever the power of injustice is triumphant peace soon degenerates into slavery.

THE VALUE OF MILITARY VIRTUE

Whatever durable peace there is or has been in the world has been produced by the better organization and direction of the innate fighting qualities of mankind. War, in spite of its terrible atrocities, has always appealed to strong and noble natures; and many of the most unselfish and useful men who have ever lived have been warriors. Calling as it does for sacrifice and heroism, conflict seems to link the individual to some great cause that lies beyond the inconsequence of mere personal ease and selfish enjoyment, and places before him an object of existence beyond himself.

So long as oppression and injustice remain in the world, there will be something worth contending for, — not necessarily, however, in any brutal sense; — and so long as there is something worth contending for, courage and fortitude will seem admirable. As the late Professor William James so truly maintained, in his essay on "The Moral Equivalent of War," the fighting impulse is a deeply rooted attribute of manhood, and needs only to be rightly directed to justify its permanent presence in the human race. But it was a great moment in the evolution of man, when the fighting impulse was redeemed from isolated outbursts of violence and brutality through its organization for tribal protection. Thenceforth, it had a definite social value. When later on it became drilled and disciplined in the person of the trained soldier, and was held in reserve for the socially determined occasion for its exercise, the fighting instinct found a new and highly advantageous direction. And, finally, when this organized power became fully responsible to civil authority, it was able to shelter peace, and made possible the development of the Modern State.

But the recognition of the value of military virtue is something very different from the apotheosis of War. No great soldier has ever glorified War, as in itself a human good. Field-Marshal Count von Moltke is often cited as writing: "Eternal peace is a dream, and not even a beautiful dream; and war is a component part in the fixed order of the universe, established by God himself. It develops man's noblest virtues of courage and renunciation, faithfulness to duty and readiness for sacrifice. Were it not for war, the world would become bemired in materialism."

We do not need to controvert this utterance of the most famous modern apologist for war, but only correctly to interpret it. These words of Count von Moltke were written, in 1880, in a letter addressed to Bluntschli, then professor of International Law at Heidelberg; who, writing as a jurist, had referred to war in terms which appeared to the great Field-Marshal unfair to the profession of a soldier.

But this apology for war by no means expressed Count von Moltke's appreciation of the inestimable value of peace. Three years earlier, on April 24, 1877, he had said in the German Reichstag: "Gentlemen, I share the hope and the wish of the orator for a lasting peace, but I do not share his confidence. Happy will be the time when the States will no longer be in a position where they must devote the greater part of their income merely to render their existence safe; and when not only the governments, but the people and parties also, shall have convinced themselves, that even a successful campaign costs more than it brings in." And only a few months before his famous letter to Bluntschli, on March

1, 1880, he made a speech in the Reichstag, in which he said: "Who could propose, by way of averting calamity, that the whole of Europe should groan under the burden of an armed peace! Mutual distrust is what keeps the nations in arms against one another. . . . All nations stand equally in need of peace."

It is evident, therefore, that Count von Moltke's apology for war was based on his conception of its necessity; and that his own ideal was a state of peace and mutual confidence between nations, if solid grounds for believing in their good will could be discovered or created.

THE RÔLE OF FORCE IN CIVILIZATION

It is quite natural, that the soldier who has devoted his life to the defence of his country and the jurist who is seeking to refer its well-being to general principles should differ not only in temperament but in the manner of regarding the same facts. The soldier looks backward, and perceives that no State has ever been able to protect the rights of its constituents which has not been prepared for self-defence against its enemies. The jurist looks forward, and hopes for a time when the process of social development will be so far advanced that men generally will see how much more advantageous it is for them to accept and obey the principles of justice than to shed one another's blood over misunderstandings. But there is no essential opposition between them. Both contemplate the same ends; but they differ as regards the means by which those ends are to be attained.

We cannot, without ignoring the facts of history, overlook the part hitherto played by armed force in the development of the Modern State. Every advance of civilization

THE STATE AS AN ARMED POWER

over barbarism and of public order over anarchy has been won by the better organization of force, and its consecration to higher purposes. The better organization of force has meant the creation of armies and navies, and their more perfect control by civil authority. The consecration of force to higher purposes has resulted in the suppression of savagery, barbarism, piracy, and despotism. To condemn armies and navies, as mere survivals of an outgrown past, while dangers to civilization still exist, would be to counsel exposure to the perils of recrudescent barbarism; for it is by no means certain, that respect for law has yet become so profound and so universal that a defenceless people may count upon the security of its rights and liberties.

On the other hand, it is not doubtful that, even among the most highly civilized peoples, there will arise differences which will somehow have to be settled between them; and, until there are trustworthy assurances that international disputes can be adjusted in some other and better way, before they have accumulated to the point of provoking armed conflict, it is morally certain that armies and navies will still have to be relied upon as guardians of peace.

It cannot, therefore, at this time, be expected, that the policy of total disarmament will be adopted by any government; nor can it be foreseen that such a policy will ever at any time be adopted. It is of the highest importance, therefore, to recognize the fact, that the element of danger in international relations does not arise from the existence of armies and navies, but from the state of mind of nations toward one another. Let us once for all make this point clear. The menace to public peace in a community does not arise from the fact that there are in the hands of the people available means of destruction which evil-minded persons might employ, but from the presence of lawlessness and the imperfect organization of justice. This is equally true of States. The extravagant increase of armed strength is owing to the conviction that, as long as principles of justice do not prevail among nations, the only security of a country lies in its effective force. The necessity for reliance upon force is, and always will be, inversely proportional to the disposition to accept and obey law. When all who are capable of inflicting injury are ready to accept and respect the authority of law, and submit without violence to the decisions of just tribunals, the rôle of force may safely be reduced to that minimum of police protection which is rendered necessary, even in a peaceful and law-abiding community, by occasional sporadic violations of personal and property rights.

The only sure path to peace is then the path of justice; and the only guarantees of justice that have yet been discovered or devised by mankind are organized force under the control of civil authority, on the one hand, and the general consent to respect the principles of justice without the application of force, on the other.

THE MOVEMENT FOR LIMITING ARMAMENTS

The practical correctness of this conclusion is instructively illustrated by the course of the movement to diminish the growth of modern armaments.

As early as 1890, Lord Salisbury is said to have been so impressed with the overgrowth of modern armaments, that he prepared for the use of the British cabinet a memorandum setting forth the heavy expenses caused by the armed peace of Europe; and this document is alleged to have been confidentially shown to at least one other Power, in the hope of

THE STATE AS AN ARMED POWER 157

convoking a European congress for the purpose of changing the situation; but the idea was abandoned without any practical result.

The "mutual distrust" which had so long existed was, however, in no respect diminished, and even appeared to be augmenting every year; for the constant increase of military preparations, unaccompanied by any plan for the better organization of international relations, placed a new emphasis on the rôle to be played by force, without giving it any justification, except the general disposition to rely upon it for security.

On August 24, 1898, the Emperor of Russia — deeply impressed with the fact, that "the moral and physical forces of the nations, labor and capital, find themselves turned aside from their natural course and consumed in a non-productive manner" by the cost of armaments — issued a circular, or rescript,[1] in which he affirmed, that "the supreme duty which imposes itself on all the States to-day consists in placing a limit to these constant armaments, and in seeking the means of escaping the calamities by which the entire world is menaced;" and to this end, he proposed to the governments having representatives accredited to the court of Russia, that a conference be called to consider this grave question.

It is worthy of note, that this first circular was confined to pointing out the economic burdens imposed by the armaments then existing and the crises that might follow a further increase of them, but by no means invited a general disarmament; nor did it propose any substitute for armed force as a guarantee of peace. Only incidentally, at the end of the

[1] The text of the Rescript and other documents relating to the First Conference at The Hague may be found in Scott, *The Hague Peace Conferences of 1889 and 1907*, II, Baltimore, 1909.

text, it was observed, that this conference of the Powers would "confirm their agreement by the solemn establishment of the principles of justice and right, upon which repose the security of States and the welfare of peoples." But the motives inspiring the proposal, as set forth in the rescript, were primarily economic, only secondarily humanitarian, and not in any exact sense juristic.

In a second circular, issued on January 11, 1899, the scope of the Conference was so defined as to include certain ameliorations in the practices of war and "the possibility of preventing armed conflicts by the pacific means at the disposal of international diplomacy"; but there was still no place indicated in the programme for the discussion of any purely juristic question; and it was declared, that "all questions concerning the political relations of States, and the order of things established by treaties, must be absolutely excluded."

Convoked and conducted as a "Peace Congress," the First International Conference at The Hague (May 18–July 29, 1899), while appealing strongly to the philanthropic sentiments of good men everywhere, awakened little real interest, and even less expectation of useful results, among practical statesmen and diplomatists. It was felt to be discourteous to a great sovereign, and ungracious toward a noble human aspiration, to oppose the movement; but, in the official world at least, it was generally referred to with ill-concealed scepticism, and sometimes with unsuppressed smiles.

Although the conference was called for the purpose of considering the subject of limiting armaments, attention was soon diverted to other matters. It was alleged by the President of the Conference, that "armed peace to-day causes more considerable expense than the most burdensome war of former times," and this statement was undisputed; but, in the brief discussion that followed, it was not generally emphasized. A study of the question of the limitation of armaments was proposed, a committee was appointed to report upon it, and, no definite plan having been presented, it was finally resolved by the Conference, "that a limitation of the military charges which now weigh upon the world is greatly to be desired in the interests of the material and moral welfare of humanity." The First Committee, to which this subject had been referred, then confined its efforts to proposals for "humanizing war."

It is fortunate that the plenipotentiaries and experts assembled at The Hague in 1899 had the good sense not to provoke a quarrel, and break up the Conference, by insisting upon a full discussion of the limitation of armaments. They perceived, that, until the "mutual distrust" which is the cause of excessive military preparations could be removed, it was impossible to obtain any agreement upon the subject; and also that too great insistence upon it would only confirm suspicions, already existing, that the proposal was not one of unadulterated philanthropy. Many of them were also of the opinion that, after all, merely dividing the cost of armies and navies into two halves, putting one half into our pockets, and using the other in the same old-fashioned way, not only did not go to the root of the matter, but would not even alter the *status quo* in any other than an economic sense.

THE ATTITUDE TOWARD INTERNATIONAL JUSTICE IN THE FIRST HAGUE CONFERENCE

The Second Committee also occupied itself with the laws and customs of war; but a Third Committee, under circumstances of great difficulty, found, or more strictly speaking created, an opportunity to give the Conference a quasi-juristic character that had not been originally contemplated. It was the work of this body that rescued the Conference from practically total failure, and set in motion a movement which registered in a convention of enduring value the farthest general advance in international conceptions attained in the nineteenth century.

The history of the manner in which this movement was initiated has never yet been fully told, nor is it necessary to relate it here. It is, however, important to note the progress made, both in the First and in the Second Hague Conferences, toward the adoption of the juristic conception of the State as the basis of future international relations.

There was, as we have seen, in the programme sent out by the Government that convoked the First Conference a proposal to consider "the possibility of preventing armed conflicts *by the pacific means at the disposal of international diplomacy.*" It was not intended that any means not at the "disposal of international diplomacy" should be employed, and these means were confined to three kinds of action: (1) good offices and mediation, (2) commissions of inquiry, and (3) occasional voluntary arbitrations. As a result of the Conference, in addition to new conventions and declarations on the laws and customs of war, there was framed a convention for the peaceful settlement of international differences, including prescriptions for the facultative use of all three of the "means at the disposal of diplomacy"; and a tribunal was provided for, to be convoked when necessary from a long list of arbitrators named by the different governments.

Great and salutary as this convention was, it did not explicitly embody in its provisions the juristic conception.

There was not one of these merely "diplomatic" means which by its terms a signatory State was not at perfect liberty to reject. Everything in this convention was purely occasional, voluntary, and therefore inconclusive. Justice was commended; but it was nowhere agreed, or even asserted, that it is obligatory upon Sovereign States.

The attitude of the Conference upon this point is unmistakable. Concessions in the interest of "peace" were recommended, and a way to make them available was provided; but nowhere was it agreed or contended that it is jurally binding upon a Sovereign State to submit any question to a tribunal of justice. A court of justice was proposed, but it was rejected. The interest of the Conference ended with provisions intended to aid in preserving "peace."

A curious illustration of this attitude is offered by the debate on the proposal to provide for a rehearing in case an error in respect of law or fact should be discovered in an arbitral decision within a limited time after the decision was rendered. It was contended that such a provision would "shipwreck the whole idea of arbitration," the purpose of which was said to be simply to end contentions rather than to secure justice. "The end of arbitration is, to terminate the controversy absolutely." On the other hand, it was contended, "Nothing is settled until it is settled right." To which it was replied, that "contracting parties *impressed from the point of view of justice* . . . should provide for a rehearing in a *special agreement;*" but evil consequences would result from making it a *general provision*, and *"the governments would risk being no longer their own masters!"* [1]

Still, although justice was subordinated to peace in the

---

[1] Holls, *The Peace Conference at The Hague*, New York, 1900, pp. 287, 303.

convention finally concluded, and both peace and justice were left without obligations, it was distinctly stated that the Conference was "*desirous* of extending the empire of law and of strengthening the sentiment of international justice"; and thus was enregistered all that was at that time possible in the form of a general agreement.

THE TRIUMPH OF THE JURISTIC IDEA IN 1907

In the Second Conference at The Hague (June 15–October 18, 1907), the programme included "improvements in the rules of the convention of 1899 for the settlement of international disputes"; but it proposed no radical extension. The limitation of armaments was not even mentioned in the programme, but the right to discuss it was reserved by a few nations, and the resolution of 1899 was confirmed by the Conference; which further declared, that it is "highly desirable to see the governments take up the serious study of the question."

That which chiefly characterized the Second Conference at The Hague, and marked the advance made in public opinion since the First, was the increased interest in the juristic idea, as contrasted with the merely pacific aspirations that prevailed in 1899. It was especially shown in the convention providing for the establishment of an international court for maritime prizes, the project for a permanent court of arbitral justice, and the agreement not to collect contractual debts by force until adjudication had been obtained, or at least proposed and refused; but, above all, in the general tenor of the discussions, in which there was manifested a bolder, firmer grasp of principles of jurisprudence as affording the true foundations of international agreements, with an evident diminution of the disposition shown in 1899 to consider Sovereign States as arbitrary entities governed by no authoritative maxims of law. The body was composed of representatives of forty-four instead of twenty-five Powers, as in the First Conference; and the debates were correspondingly wider in scope, more extended in form, and represented a greater diversity of view. Although the procedure was far more in accordance with diplomatic than with parliamentary usages, the note of jurisprudence was accentuated above that of diplomacy, which throughout the Conference was more busied with obstruction than with leadership.

It was recognized on all sides, that arbitration had taken great steps in advance in the previous eight years, and that it had "conquered its *droit de cité* in the world"; for four important cases had been settled at The Hague, and thirty-three arbitration treaties had been signed. It was admitted by all, that improvements in the previous convention were necessary; and thirty-two Powers were in favor of compulsory arbitration with regard to certain classes of disputes.

It is not necessary here to follow in detail the efforts to establish the permanent court of arbitral justice, the project of which was published in the Final Act of the Conference, nor to recite the causes of its failure to be adopted. But that which is important to note is, *that no objection was raised to it in principle.* No voice was lifted in defence of the idea, now left apparently without defenders, that it is beneath the dignity of Sovereign States to present their differences on any subject where a principle of right is involved to the decision of neutral judges, whose function is not merely to find an acceptable *via media* between them in a diplomatic sense, but to determine what is just in a judicial sense.

THE JURISTIC CONCEPTION NOT YET ORGANIZED

Here then is the final triumph of the juristic conception of the State as a question of principle. In the open forum of public discussion this conception stands unassailed; or at least without an avowed opponent among the delegates of the forty-four Sovereign States represented at the Second Hague Conference, the first universal congress in the history of the world.

It is true, that that conception has not yet taken the organic form which it requires, in order to render it effective in the sphere of practice; but it has attained a victory in the moral and intellectual realm which must be recognized as one of the great achievements of the human race. It would be inappropriate for any man or any country to boast, that this triumph has been obtained through this or that particular initiative, or this or that specific argument, as if the result were the effect of any of these. It is, in fact, the mere bringing to clear immediate consciousness of a truth that has been latent in every human mind that has busied itself with the real nature of the State since that great question became an object of reflective thought. The question of peace is and always has been the question of justice, and nothing else. Wherever there is perfect justice there is peace, and wherever there is serious injustice there is a reason for conflict until it is removed. Peace was never broken except by an unjust act; and war in principle is never ended until injustice is ended, or men are beaten into submission to it. While injustice endures, the best men will consider it a duty to fight; and they will inevitably prepare to fight. The only true peace consists in the triumph of right over injustice. This is the human ideal which the Modern State was created to realize, and until it is fully realized the nations will continue to arm themselves against their enemies, real or imaginary, as the case may be.

THE WARLIKE MAINTENANCE OF PEACE

We are often told, that the best conceivable guarantee of peace is preparation for war.

In the case of a particular country exposed to attack by a definite enemy, preparation for war, if sufficient to discourage attack, may serve to postpone, or even to avert, the conflict; but it evidently does not do so by removing the cause. When both sides are equally prepared, the cause still existing, the probability of a conflict is rendered even greater; for the reason that each side, relying upon its armed strength, will be the less disposed to seek some method of reasonable conciliation, and the struggle may thus become inevitable.

But the sophistical character of this doctrine, that peace is promoted by preparation for war, appears perfectly clear when it is applied in a general sense, and all nations undertake to maintain peace by rivalry in augmenting their military strength; for, on every side, there is thereby created that "mutual distrust" which, according to Count von Moltke, "is what keeps the nations in arms against one another." If, as this great authority affirms, the cause of armament is "mutual distrust," it is obvious, that the general augmentation of military strength, which constantly increases distrust, can never become a sufficient guarantee of peace. The whole development moves in a vicious circle; for distrust increases armament, armament increases distrust, and so on *ad infinitum*.

But, evident as the pernicious influence of this doctrine

may be in theory, it becomes even more so in the sphere of practice. The overgrowth of armaments, considered from the international point of view, creates a constant menace to the world's peace, because of the diplomatic complications it engenders. When a nation has strained its resources to the utmost in order to equal its neighbor's military strength, failing in that endeavor, it seeks to enter into alliances with other nations against its rival; not because it has suffered any definite ill-treatment by him, but simply because it fears the use he may make of his superior power. Thus begins the fatal procedure of secret understandings, and the still more fatal suspicion that these exist where they do not exist, until the whole civilized world is enmeshed in a net-work of diplomatic intrigues, or is perturbed by the apprehension that these are being carried on. Espionage follows; half-truths are discovered and exaggerated; suspicion ripens into conviction; and the whole earth seems undermined with plots and counterplots, until frank and loyal friendship is made impossible.

The truth is, that the progress of civilization has been promoted by the organization of force under civil control, but never by mere military force alone. When military force exists beyond the means of effective civil organization, it becomes a menace, even to those supposed to control it. And here two great facts have to be considered.

The first is, that nothing is so perilous as a secret organization of force, and especially in international relations. Again and again, it has been proved, that secret international arrangements for the combination of forces are for the most part illusory. When the issue comes, not all the allies are equally affected; and the assurances that have been relied upon often entirely fail in the moment of need. Where combinations have been made partly through compulsion, they are usually utterly worthless. The weak are, as a rule, only too well pleased to promote the isolation of the strong; and isolation, whenever it is possible, is what the strong who resort to violence have naturally to expect.

The other fact is, that public force beyond the actual needs of the State, that is, force in excess of what is justified by public necessity, is in itself a menace to the State. Within a few months, we have seen the revolt of armies and navies; and in widely separated countries, we have witnessed the surprising phenomenon of public forces dictating to established governments the terms of their service and obedience. These occurrences are not so infrequent as to be entirely exceptional. And what is the logical inference from them? Is it not, that military force alone cannot be relied upon to serve the purposes of the State, but only civilly organized force? What then is "civilly organized force"? It is force related to the needs of law and order, permeated by the ideas of law and order, and held responsible to them by sustained civil authority. Without this, the Modern State becomes impossible; and any augmentation of public force beyond the public needs, and long continued separation of it from the jural consciousness of the nation must inevitably tend to render the State less potential in the accomplishment of its purpose.

THE PEACEFUL REGULATION OF WAR

It marks a new epoch in the relations of Sovereign States that, in spite of the increase of preparation for war, peace is now considered the normal condition, which great armaments are intended to maintain. New emphasis is given to the transitory character of the warlike maintenance of peace by the peaceful efforts for the regulation of war. It is now universally admitted, that the only justification for armed conflict is the necessity of settling questions which cannot be determined otherwise.

It is agreed that all unnecessary cruelty and injustice are to be eliminated, the rights of non-combatants are to be respected, and those of neutrals safeguarded. For these purposes, rules of action have been adopted by practically all civilized States relating to the opening of hostilities, the laws and customs of war on land, the rights and duties of neutral powers and persons, the treatment of an enemy's merchant vessels at the beginning of hostilities, the transformation of merchant ships into vessels of war, the placing of submarine mines, bombardment of naval forces, adaptation to maritime war of the principles of the Geneva Convention, the restriction of the right of capture in maritime warfare, and a declaration regarding the throwing of projectiles and explosives from balloons. These are some of the results of The Hague Conferences, to which are to be added the proposal of an international prize court on the basis of a naval code worked out by the Maritime Powers in the Conference of London (December 4, 1908, to February 26, 1909).

These results, arrived at by the coöperation of military and naval experts, sitting in council under the instructions of their governments, show that war is henceforth to be regulated by definite rules, and it is agreed that even in moments of deadly combat the juristic character of the State is henceforth to be recognized and respected.

By placing armies and navies under the regulation of international rules of justice, the arbitrary assumption that Sovereign States are superior to all law is effectually silenced. Henceforth, war cannot be conducted by any civilized nation without at least a nominal respect for the laws of war. But, if this be so, can any civilized nation hereafter permit itself to begin a war without a previous attempt to apply the principles of justice, since it is bound to respect them in conducting its operations?

The peaceful regulation of war leads logically to the judicial organization of peace; for, if principles of justice are worthy of respect, and nations willingly bind themselves to respect them in the conduct of warlike operations, are they not equally worthy of consideration in securing the preservation of peace?

The successful efforts for "humanizing war" — cynical as the expression may sound — go far toward proving the possibility of "humanizing" the permanent relations of peace; for they illustrate the practicability of restricting the unbridled liberties of primitive times by subjecting the employment of force to regulations possessing the character of law. But, if the operations of war may be thus regulated by principles of justice and mercy, may not its preliminaries also, without loss to national dignity, be subjected to similar regulations? If soldiers and sailors, in the heat of mortal combat, when blood is flowing and life hangs in the balance, are expected to observe rules of conduct laid down for them in international conventions, should not diplomatists and statesmen also be subject to reasonable rules of procedure before deciding that it is necessary for these men to expose their lives in battle?

THE JUDICIAL ORGANIZATION OF PEACE

If war were the best or the only means of obtaining justice, our jural consciousness might be satisfied by leaving each State to resort to it without restriction; but it requires little reflection to make it plain, that physical conflict has in it no element whatever that can be described as determinative of justice. There is in the chances of battle no standard of proportion between the wrong to be redressed and the amount of injury inflicted, and no relation whatever between the rights to be established and the preponderance of force by which victory is decided. The only issue of the struggle is a temporary settlement of the question, who at that time is the stronger; and whose will, whether right or wrong, shall prevail.

The expression "temporary settlement" has been deliberately chosen, for mere physical contest is seldom a final settlement of any question between nations. In general, not only the original cause of opposition remains undiminished, but new grounds of hostility are thereby engendered; leaving a permanent animosity that takes the form of hereditary hatred, often too deeply implanted to be removed by argument or conciliation, and therefore indefinitely persistent.

When, in primitive times, men contended over their rights body to body, with the naked sword in hand, there was perhaps the feeling that he who was in the right, by inviting the judgment of God in a trial of strength, would be sustained in that appeal by the justice of his cause; and that he who was in the wrong, when he looked into the eyes of him whom he had injured, would be condemned as unworthy in his own heart, so that his force would fail through the reproaches of his own conscience. But there is nothing in modern warfare to cause a guilty soul to quail before the face of innocence. There is no longer even any battle-line of crouching infantry and dashing cavalry, where bayonets and sabres meet and clash till they drip with crimson. A rain of singing bullets, propelled by smokeless powder, aimed by invisible marksmen, falls upon the open field. A distant crest is surmounted with machine guns that mow the meadow over which the charge must be made, as a reaper gathers the ripened grain. Great explosive shells drop from mathematically calculated points in the sky, to rend the earth and every living thing upon it with gaping wounds. Victory in modern war is less than ever a matter of personal achievement; and has become an affair determined by the number of men, the size and quality of guns, and above all by the ability to borrow money to pay the cost.

The judicial organization of peace may present greater difficulties than the humanization of war, for the reason that war is a physical process, consisting in overcoming one set of forces by another set of forces; while peace is a condition, involving the adjustment of a vast variety of conflicting rights and interests; but all the more, and for this very reason, it is necessary that intelligence, rather than force, should be employed in effecting this adjustment. When men did not yet possess clear notions of their rights, and there was no organized protection for them, it was but natural that single questions should be settled by the direct use of force; but now that rights are more effectively protected by organized power, it is evident how ill adapted the application of force has become to accomplish the ends of justice. When we consider how much injustice and unmerited injury even a just war of necessity inflicts upon the innocent, we cannot escape the conclusion that the test of battle is at best but a crude and cumbrous method of settling differences which might be better determined in some other way.

PROFIT AND LOSS IN WAR

It is extremely doubtful if the interests of the State, and especially the interests of those who compose the population, are on the whole well served by a war of aggression, even when it is successful. In his book, "The Great Illusion," [1] Norman Angell has undertaken to prove: (1) that armaments do not pay, because the minor Powers, with feeble armaments, enjoy better financial credit — their government bonds selling at higher prices — than the great military Powers; (2) that war indemnities do not pay, because the relations of trade are disturbed by the transfer of great sums from one country to another, unfavorably for the recipient; (3) that annexations do not pay, because the cost of assimilating them is not repaid by the excess of taxes derived from them; and (4) that war in general does not pay, because the financial interdependence of Modern States is such that property cannot be confiscated on a large scale without a disturbance of trade and credit that would seriously injure the industry and finance of the conquering country.

This subject is too large to be satisfactorily considered here; but, whatever the relative merits of peace and war may be, when considered from a financial point of view, the resort to war merely for purposes of gain would be incompatible with the nature and purposes of the Modern State, and could not receive the approval of any civilized nation.

And yet it is constantly assumed, that the conflicting interests of Great Powers are in some mysterious way bearing them on, as by an irresistible under-current, to some awful catastrophe, for which the nations must prepare. It has been recently said, and by a high authority: "The weak man cannot

[1] Angell, *The Great Illusion*, London, 1910.

trust his judge, and the dream of the peace advocate is nothing but a dream!"

Whom then shall the "weak man" trust? Shall he trust the strong man, rather than the just judge? But whom shall the strong man trust? Shall he trust no one but himself? What then is to become of the State? How, upon this theory, shall the State demand of the strong man, as well as of the weak man, obedience to its laws? It is time to realize, that dependence upon force, without regard to law and justice, implies a return to anarchy, and the subversion of the State. The refusal of the State to be just, because it is strong, would be a repudiation of the principles upon which its authority is founded.

IS WAR INEVITABLE?

But why is the aspiration of the "peace advocate" declared to be "nothing but a dream"? Is it true, that peace is only a dream, and war the reality? Do not the periods of peace exceed in duration the periods of war? Which then is the dream, and which the reality? When it is considered, that the price of a single battleship has never yet been expended by all the nations of the earth combined for the judicial organization of peace, is it not at least premature to say, that further progress in this direction is impossible?

Who then is prepared to maintain the inevitability of war among really civilized nations? How many times have the prophets of evil cried out in their nightmare, "There will be war!" and yet the crisis has passed, the misunderstanding has been cleared up, the rightful concession has been made, and there has been no war. And what proof is there, that war between civilized States is inevitable? Is it not better to avoid dogmatism, and confine ourselves to the discussion of admitted facts?

This much, at least, is certain, that it lies within the power of the great juristic States to determine the question of war and peace; and it may be said, with equal certainty, that there is no Great Power which desires to engage in war with any other. The chief real danger lies in preparing the minds of men for war, rather than for peace. There are many purely private interests that promote the belief that war is inevitable, and that nations must prepare for it; but, regarded from the point of view of public interest, this belief, that war is inevitable, has very frail support. In the days of wide-spread superstition, it was easy to make men believe that human destinies were determined by mysterious powers over which the intelligence of man had no control; but the time has gone by when the convictions of civilized nations can be influenced by such beliefs. There are in the world to-day no demonstrable rights or interests, as between well-organized Modern States, which may not be adjusted without bloodshed; and it would be difficult to point out any advantage that could be gained by any one of them over the others that would compensate for the losses of life and money that would be occasioned by war between them. Their one common enemy has been already pointed out and branded. His name is Mutual Distrust. He cannot be overcome by quick-firing guns, or aeroplanes charged with explosives, or fleets of battleships. There is but one champion able to destroy him. In the right hand is the uplifted sword, but it is broken; in the other trembles the balance, which has not been tried. Yet it is before this august presence of Justice that the nations must learn their destiny.

VIII

THE STATE AS A JUSTICIABLE PERSON

HAVING organized peace within its own borders, by substituting the reign of law for discord and violence, it is only by denaturing itself and reverting to a less perfect type of social existence, that the Constitutional State can disregard the principles of justice, and lend itself to violence in its relations with other States.

It is not, however, to be expected that the judicial organization of peace, in an international sense, can be accomplished in any other than the gradual manner in which its internal triumphs have been achieved; and account must also be taken of the serious obstacles it has to overcome in the traditions and inheritances with which it is embarrassed.

THE EVOLUTION OF ORGANIZED JUSTICE

The system of public order within the State, based on judicial institutions, has been of extremely slow development. Even in the early period of Roman history, there appears to have been nothing like a modern court of justice. When disputes arose, arbitrators were called in; but permanent judges were unknown. The submission of a case to arbitrators was by special contract, in which the litigants promised to abide by the decision. In time, a body of professional arbitrators was designated; but, we are assured by competent authorities, it was not until the period of the Empire that official courts were established at Rome, furnished with official judges, whose decisions were enforced and executed by the authority of the State.

That men found it possible to live for a long time without the benefit of duly organized justice, is further illustrated by the conditions that existed in England as late as the year 1166, when Henry II instituted his great legal reforms. There had been a long period of violence when the king substituted for the unequal authority of the local magnates judges and officers of his own appointment. The royal courts then became the refuge of the people. By the establishment of judicial circuits and the introduction of the jury into the procedure of the courts, royal justice was brought to the doors of the whole nation. The nobles complained of the innovation; but the kingdom, which had been the scene of incredible crime and discord, seriously retarding its economic development, was thereby placed upon the highway of prosperity.

Little as we may admire the spirit of imperialism represented by the Napoleonic conquests, it is not to be denied, that many of the States of the European continent derived similar benefits from the legal and judicial reforms introduced by Napoleon I. At the beginning of the nineteenth century, torture was still practiced as a method of judicial procedure; a multitude of small States retained their clumsy local laws based on feudal custom, and these were administered in the most arbitrary manner.

When we consider how slow and how difficult the progress of judicial organization within the State has been, it is not surprising that, in an international sense, it has long seemed impossible to human powers. And the magnitude of this undertaking is rendered still more impressive, when we remember how the conception of justice itself has been retarded. It seems to us to-day almost incredible, that prosecutions for the wholly imaginary crime of witchcraft should have continued down to the year 1793, and that, in a single century, and a single country, more than a hundred thousand victims were burned to death, after confessing, under torture, to such impossible offences as riding through the air on broom-sticks, signing compacts with Satan, and even bearing children to him. So firm was the belief in the existence of these impossibilities, of the rectitude of obtaining evidence by torture, and of the perfect justice of punishing these imaginary crimes by the most barbarous form of death, that the great German jurist, Thomasius, did not dare to publish his convictions on the subject, or to go farther than to question the sufficiency of the evidence of Satan's part in these performances.[1]

If there be one clear lesson that history has to teach us, it is, that arguments based upon time-honored practices and convictions, untested by modern knowledge and judgment, are utterly worthless in any branch of science; and most of all in morality and jurisprudence, which are so difficult to test and so profoundly influenced by dogmatic authority. When witches were no longer tortured into the confession of falsehoods, but given a fair chance for life in an open court, face to face with their accusers, it presently became evident that there were no longer any witches. The better organization of justice emptied the Brocken of its midnight orgies, and proved that good men, in the name of religion, had for centuries practiced cruelties that fill our minds with horror.

[1] White, *Seven Great Statesmen*, New York, 1910, pp. 113, 161.

THE RIGHT OF WAR

There are, at the present time in many different countries, considerable numbers of excellent men who believe the settlement of international disputes by warlike rather than by judicial methods to be quite as irrational as trial by torture, and as cruel toward the innocent as execution for witchcraft.

The writers on International Law, seeing that the "right" of Sovereign States to declare and wage war has generally been accepted without dissent, have often rather arrogantly swept aside the protest against war as a kind of impertinence, emanating from sentimental persons who do not fully comprehend what they are talking about.

As an illustration of this attitude, take the following statement by one of the most recent and highly esteemed of the living writers on this subject: "Fanatics of international peace," says Dr. Oppenheim, "as well as those innumerable individuals who cannot grasp the idea of a law between Sovereign States, frequently consider war and law inconsistent." [1]

"It is not difficult," he then proceeds to say, "to show the absurdity of this opinion. As States are Sovereign, and as consequently no central authority can exist above them able to enforce compliance with its demands, war cannot always be avoided. International Law recognizes this fact, but at the same time provides regulations with which the belligerents have to comply. . . . International Law does not and cannot object to the States which are in conflict waging war upon each other, instead of peaceably settling their difference. But if they choose to go to war, they have to comply with the rules laid down by International Law regarding the conduct of war and the relations between belligerents and neutral States."

[1] Oppenheim, *International Law*, London, 1905, II, p. 55.

THE STATE AS A JUSTICIABLE PERSON 179

It is to be feared that the persons for whose benefit this passage is intended may be more bewildered than enlightened by it. They are told, on the one hand, that no central authority can exist "able to enforce compliance with its demands"; and, on the other, that International Law "provides regulations with which the belligerents have to comply." Why do belligerents "have to comply" with these regulations? For no other reason than that they have *agreed* to do so. But, if International Law may, by agreement, provide regulations with which belligerents have to comply regarding the operations of war, why may it not, by a similar agreement, provide regulations also regarding the preliminaries of war, namely, its proper causes and conditions?

The most that can be said in reply is, that Sovereign States have so far made no agreement upon this subject. As will be seen a little later, this is not precisely true; for at least one important limitation to the alleged "right of war" has been agreed to by practically all Sovereign States. While, therefore, with the exception just referred to, it cannot be affirmed that International Law has so far placed any limit to the "right of war"; it cannot, on the other hand, be maintained that every Sovereign State has a "legal right" to make war on whom and for whatever cause it pleases. The truth is, there is no law on the subject.

It cannot it is true be said that "war and law are inconsistent," but it may be asserted that there is an inconsistency between an unlimited right of war and the principles of justice, which is what the alleged "fanatics" have in mind; and this is admitted by the author just cited, who says: "If International Law could forbid war altogether, it would be a more perfect law than it is at present."

"Theoretically," says one of the most eminent of recent

authorities on the subject, the late William Edward Hall, "International Law ought to determine the causes for which war can be justly undertaken; in other words, it ought to mark out as plainly as municipal law what constitutes a wrong for which a remedy may be sought at law. It might also not unreasonably go on to discourage the commission of wrongs by investing a State seeking redress with special rights, and by subjecting a wrong-doer to special disabilities." But, in fact, it does nothing of this kind. "However able law might be," he goes on to say, "to declare one of two combatants to have committed a wrong, it would be idle for it to affect to impart the character of a penalty to war, when it is powerless to enforce its decisions. The obedience which is paid to law must be a willing obedience, and when a State has taken up arms unjustly it is useless to expect it to acquiesce in the imposition of penalties for its act. International Law has consequently no alternative but to accept war, independently of the justice of its origin, as a relation which the parties to it may set up if they choose, and to busy itself only in regulating the effects of the relation. Hence, both parties to every war are regarded as being in an identical position, and consequently being possessed of equal rights." [1]

Thus far then International Law has confined itself to making rules for the conduct of war, but has not ventured to lay down rules for determining the question whether or not a particular war is legal. Both parties, the aggressor and the defender, are considered as possessing the same rights.

To appreciate how little justice there is in this, let us try to comprehend precisely what is meant by "war"; and, with that in view, let us take Dr. Oppenheim's excellent definition of it, which is, "A contention between two or more States,

[1] Hall, *A Treatise on International Law*, Oxford, 1895, pp. 63, 64.

THE STATE AS A JUSTICIABLE PERSON

through their armed forces, for the purpose of overpowering each other, and imposing such conditions of peace as the victor pleases." By this definition, to which no objection can be made, the right to declare and wage war implies the unlimited power of one State to impose its will, as far as its armed force enables it to do so, upon another State.

Whence did the State obtain this "right"? The question is not, Whence did the State obtain the right to defend its territory from attack, or to use force to secure justice not to be secured in some other way? but, Whence did it obtain the right to attack another State, for any reason it may regard as sufficient, or for no reason but its own volition?

THE FALLACY OF THE ABSOLUTE RIGHT OF WAR

It is, first of all, to be noted, that this alleged "right" is reserved exclusively to a Sovereign State. It is, therefore, from the attribute of "sovereignty" — to which we have already given some attention — that the "right of war," with the permission to take life, destroy property, impose indemnities for the costs of a campaign, annex territory, and other like prerogatives, is supposed to be derived.

When we have reduced the reasoning on which the "right" of war is based to its lowest terms, we find that it amounts to this: Sovereignty, or supreme power, is the source of all the rights possessed by the State. Among these is the right to use force; which, being an attribute of "supreme power," cannot in any way be limited as respects its purpose, object, or authority. It can be limited, in fact, only by the opposition of a greater force; in which case, when overcome, it ceases to be "supreme," and must submit to the superior power that has overcome it, which then takes the place, and consequently the "rights," of supremacy, since it has proved itself in reality "supreme."

The real problem for jurisprudence is, however, to bring this little system of mechanics into relation to anything that a human being can call a "right," for a "right" can never be derived from mere "power"; but, on the assumption that Might makes Right, it is all very easy; and, as we have seen, that was the assumption when Bodin invented his famous doctrine of sovereignty.

But, as Jellinek has clearly pointed out, this abstract idea of *suprema potestas*, or supreme power, is, in reality, a purely *negative* idea.[1] It possesses no positive, definite, concrete content whatever. What can be meant by *supremacy*, taken in its abstract sense, except that there exists *nothing* superior to it? And, if we put the emphasis on the bare idea of *power*, we have before our minds merely the most general idea of efficiency, and nothing more. If, again, it be insisted, that we must take the two words together, what then, in any definable terms, can be meant by "supreme power," except that it is power than which there is no greater? But this statement is merely exclusive and not in any sense comprehensive, for no one could affirm that "supreme power," as possessed by the State, means *all* power; for if it did, the State could create worlds, or render men immortal, as easily as it could make laws!

It would be incomprehensible that the whole theory of the State, and many of the conceptions of International Law, could ever have been built up on this empty formula, if history did not explain in what manner positive and concrete contents were read into this abstract concept of "sovereignty." But, historically regarded, it becomes very plain.

---

[1] Jellinek, *Allgemeine Staatslehre*, p. 439.

THE STATE AS A JUSTICIABLE PERSON

Bodin identified the State with the absolute ruler; and all the concrete *powers* — which were then, without any evidence, regarded also as *rights* — exercised by an absolute ruler were at once treated as if they were included in the "supreme power" in which "sovereignty" was represented to consist. Since that time, every form of the State which has regarded itself as the heir of "sovereignty" has taken over, and considered as its "rights," the "powers" formerly exercised by an absolute ruler.

Among these powers is, of course, the alleged "right" of war, formerly undisputed in the case of a sovereign, though claimed also even by non-sovereign persons in the time when Bodin's theory of sovereignty was formed, but reserved by his theory as a *privilege* belonging exclusively to the sovereign representing the "supreme" power.

How inconsequent the pretensions based on the argument for the "right" of war, as derived directly from absolute "sovereignty," really are, is evident the moment we think of the changes that since the sixteenth century have taken place in the conception of the State. In the modern conception, the State, as an embodiment of law based on guarantees, has in it no absolute element whatever. Every power the State possesses is conceived of as relative and limited, and this limitation is defined by constitutional provisions. The Modern State recognizes *no superior;* but it recognizes *equals*, both among its own constitutional organs, and in the society of States of which it is a member. It is autonomous when regarded from within, and independent when regarded from without; but for absolutism, which it has repudiated, it has substituted the limitations implied in a coördination of powers.

THE PRINCIPLE OF INVIOLABILITY

But the Constitutional State — and nearly all Modern States now claim to be constitutional — has placed in the foreground another and more fundamental principle than that of absolutism, by which the idea of unlimited power is neutralized. This is the principle of *the inviolability of the innocent person*.

If we pause to inquire what it is that most essentially characterizes the entire constitutional movement, we find that it is the idea that every person possesses inherent rights which the State must recognize and which it exists to protect, not from external enemies alone but from injury by the organs of the State itself. The right and the duty of forcible restraint and of punishment, where wrong has been inflicted, are, of necessity, inherent in the powers of the State; but the immunity of the innocent from the exercise of public power against life, liberty, and property is guaranteed by the organic laws from which the Modern State derives its being and authority.

In contrast with the wholesale renunciation of personal rights which had to be endured under the unlimited powers of the Absolute State, the Constitutional State is a system of defined and coördinated authority, based upon the idea of personal rights, and constructed for the purpose of securing their protection.

It is evident that the principle of inviolability, thus incorporated in the Modern State, has a determining influence upon the interpretation of sovereignty. It would be absurd to profess that a State thus constituted possesses the "right," without due cause, to overpower another State, and impose such conditions of peace as the victor pleases. The State, as a juristic person, is bound by the laws of its own being to claim for itself, and to accord to other States of like character, the inviolability of innocence, which is its most fundamental postulate.

The "right" of war is, therefore, a limited right, and does not exist, unless it is necessary to employ force in order to obtain the recognition of a right denied or to redress a wrong inflicted. It is true, that International Law has not in terms defined the conditions upon which war may be legally declared and prosecuted; and, in the absence of an agreement upon that subject, it may be said, that every form of injustice in the aims and purposes of war may be practiced without formal illegality; but it cannot be contended, that a Modern State does not do violence to its own nature, and in effect repudiate its own constructive principles, if it enters upon a war that is not just.

It is evident, further, that the principle of the inviolability of the innocent is as worthy of recognition, and of being established by means of solemn guarantees in the Law of Nations, as in the constitution of separate States; and that the same interest ought to be felt, and the same activity exercised, in the wider as in the narrower field.

If a law upon this subject were now to be made, in accordance with the nature of the Modern State and with the principles upon which it is founded, it is evident what such a law would logically have to be. Every Sovereign State maintains its own inviolability as essential to its independence, and it is an established principle of International Law that all Sovereign States are juridically equal; from which it follows, that, in principle, the inviolability of all Sovereign States is universally admitted. But, if this is true, there is no "right" of war in the sense of a right to overpower by force of arms a Sovereign State, and impose upon it such conditions of peace as the victor pleases. A Sovereign State has no right to take up arms against another, unless a right has been denied or an injury inflicted by it, for which reparation cannot otherwise be obtained; and it has no "right," which any Modern State could consistently recognize, in any case, to impose such arbitrary conditions of peace *as the victor pleases*. It may, in fact, commit such an act of violence, and inflict any conceivable measure of injustice; but it would be destructive of the whole conception of right, to maintain that such an excess is legally justified. There never has been, and there never could be, a general consent to the principle, that one State may rightly thus enforce its unlimited will upon another.

THE RESPONSIBILITY OF THE STATE

On the other hand, it is evident that the State is responsible for its conduct; for immunity from unjust attack implies the obligation of just treatment, and it would be absurd to consider an injurious State as sheltered from justice by the principle of inviolability. As Sir Sherston Baker has well said: "The obligation of a State to render justice is a *perfect* obligation, of strictly binding force, at all times and under all circumstances. No State can relieve itself from this obligation, under any pretext whatever." [1]

The material differences between States may seem, at first thought, to necessitate a difference in the measure of their rights and duties. We quite naturally believe that a great State, with a numerous population, has a just claim to a larger space for expansion and a greater influence in the commerce of the world than a little State; for it is evident, that

[1] Baker, *First Steps in International Law*, London, 1889, p. 158.

a strong Power possesses attributes which do not belong to a weak one. In some respects, this is undeniable; and it would seem quite right, that a great maritime Power, like Great Britain, for example, should have a larger share in determining the rules to be observed upon the sea, either in peace or war, than an exclusively inland State, like Bolivia, for example, which possesses no maritime interests.

It is also true, that there are various degrees of preparation among States for asserting their rights and discharging their obligations. It may even be said, that, since the juristic conception of the State has only in recent times obtained recognition and a degree of realization, there must be some political communities that are not yet sufficiently consolidated and developed to accept it. There are new States, and also some old ones, still passing through a period of change, which might not be able to depend upon the firm support of their own constituents in assuming the obligations and performing the duties which would be required by principles of strict international justice.

As between such undeveloped political communities, it may still be practically impossible to accept and apply a more perfect form of international justice than that which already exists. For these States, no doubt, there are many questions that must be settled as such questions have always been settled, namely, by a struggle for existence, in the form of conflict between unyielding purposes. Nations have been formed by a process of evolution that must perhaps go on; because it is the only way by which responsible States can be brought into being, and for these communities much painful discipline may still be necessary, in order to create in them the qualities of self-reliance that form the essential substance of a Modern State.

But leaving these imperfect political communities out of account, until they are fully equipped with the internal stability necessary to render external guarantees effective, there exist Powers which have attained mature development, complete self-mastery, and absolute responsibility. These are prepared — and by their spirit of justice, moderation, and mutual friendship have proved that they are prepared — to exchange guarantees of peace based on guarantees of justice. No question of life or death is likely to arise between them. They are bound together by common moral and economic interests, and by the acceptance of great principles of jurisprudence which they all constantly apply.

THE SUBORDINATION OF THE STATE TO JUDICIAL PRINCIPLES

There has been in the past few decades a gradual recognition of the fact that it is no derogation to the sovereignty of a Constitutional State to submit the question of its rights and duties to impartial judicial decision.

In commenting upon the Constitution of the United States, Mr. Justice Story long ago pointed out, that, liberal as the provisions of our fundamental law are in carrying out the intention "to establish justice," mentioned in the preamble, a citizen who has suffered wrong at the hands of the United States cannot bring his grievance before the courts, and must await, if he secures justice at all, the tardy action of the legislative branch. He contrasts this with the broader provision of the British Constitution, upon which he observes: "In England, if any person has, in point of property, a just demand upon the king, he may petition him in his court of chancery (by what is called a petition of right) where the chancellor will administer right, theoretically as a matter of grace, and not upon compulsion; but, in fact, as a matter of constitutional duty." And the learned commentator adds: "Surely it can afford no pleasant source of reflection to an American citizen, proud of his rights and privileges, that in a monarchy the judiciary is clothed with ample powers to give redress to the humblest subject in a matter of private contract or property against the Crown, and that in a republic there is an utter denial of justice in such cases to any citizen through the instrumentality of any judicial process. He may complain, but he cannot compel a hearing. The republic enjoys a despotic sovereignty to act or refuse to act as it may please, and is placed beyond the reach of law. The monarch bows to the law, and is compelled to yield his prerogative at the footstool of justice."[1]

It is evident, that the distinguished jurist just quoted considered the conception of sovereignty embodied in our Constitution as in this respect overstrained; and that it would have been more in harmony with the claims of justice, and a more perfect recognition of "constitutional duty," if provision for the redress of wrongs done by the State had been made by referring them to a court. It was, however, more for the sake of convenience in practice than from a different conception of duty, that the framers of our Constitution omitted this provision. It was never doubted by them that a wrong done by the State to a private person should in some way be righted, but it was left to the Congress to make that reparation in each case; for that body, equally with the Judiciary, represents the sovereignty of the nation, and its action, like that of the English chancellor, is an act of "constitutional duty" performed in another manner. But experi-

[1] Story, *Commentaries on the Constitution of the United States*, II, pp. 475, 478.

ence has shown, that, for this purpose, it is desirable to have a properly constituted tribunal of justice; and accordingly by Act of February 24, 1855, a Court of Claims was established at Washington, and constituted in its present form by the Act of 1863, with subsequent amendments.

Most civilized countries, including all of the Great Powers, have sufficiently developed their sense of jural responsibility to submit questions of national obligation not only to their own municipal courts, but to international tribunals; and, having taken this step, they find that they have in no way impaired their autonomy or independence. We may, therefore, with the most perfect assurance, dismiss the idea that submission by a Sovereign State to the decision of an international court is in the least derogatory to its sovereignty.[1]

THE PROGRESS OF INTERNATIONAL JUSTICE

Thus, by almost imperceptible stages, the Modern State has come to recognize the fact that it is not only a juristic but a justiciable person. It is an ancient maxim of the Law of Nations that a Sovereign State is not amenable to a suit at law *without its own consent;* but it has never been held that it is in any respect derogatory to the dignity of a State to appear before a court of justice, to answer for its conduct and meet its responsibilities, provided in doing so it acted freely.

And Modern States have not only repeatedly appeared before judges, but it has now become a custom to do so. Matters of great moment, involving not only vast sums of money but great legal principles, have been adjudicated in this way. The dispute between the United States and Great

---

[1] See the clear statement on this point by Professor Philipp Zorn, *Das Deutsche Reich und die Internationale Schiedsgerichtbarkeit*, Berlin, 1911.

Britain regarding the Alabama Claims was one of the first great cases disposed of in this manner. The history of the development of international arbitration, with a full digest of the cases to which the United States has been a party down to 1898, has been published in a monumental work by a distinguished professor in this University;[1] but it was not until the First Hague Conference, in 1899, that the movement assumed a strictly international and organized form. In the first five years after that Conference, sixty-three international disputes were referred to arbitral settlement.[2] Previous to the Second Hague Conference, thirty-three separate treaties of "obligatory" arbitration for certain classes of cases were registered in the Bureau of the Administrative Council of the Permanent Court of Arbitration at The Hague. Two of these conventions stipulate obligatory arbitration for *all* differences, *without exception*.[3] Since the Second Hague Conference, the number of arbitral agreements has greatly increased; and, at the end of the year 1909, it had grown to two hundred and eighty-eight.

The Second Hague Conference discussed at length the project of a general convention for compulsory arbitration; but, while the Conference was "unanimous in recognizing the *principle* of obligatory arbitration," and the delegations of thirty-two countries were in favor of it in certain cases, — only nine being opposed, and three abstaining from voting, — it proved impossible to secure unanimity for the project.[4]

[1] Moore, *History and Digest of the International Arbitrations to Which the United States Has been a Party*, Washington, 1898.
[2] Darby, *Modern Pacific Settlements*, London, 1904, pp. 134, 153.
[3] These were between Denmark and the Netherlands, Feb. 12, 1904; and between Denmark and Italy, Dec. 16, 1905.
[4] Those voting against in the Committee of Examination were: Germany, Austria-Hungary, Belgium, Bulgaria, Greece, Montenegro, Roumania, Switzerland, and Turkey; those abstaining were: Italy, Japan, and Luxemburg. All the others were in favor of the draft convention.

While, therefore, it cannot be said that compulsory arbitration has been universally accepted for any class of cases; it is not to be doubted, that, in those of a strictly legal character, and not affecting national "honor" or "vital interests," arbitration would be voluntarily resorted to by most civilized nations, without the menace of an appeal to arms.

But the real significance of recent progress regarding international justice is not to be found in either the general or the special obligations thus far officially assumed by Modern States. It is to be found rather in the uncontested juristic character of international rights and duties. It is easy to understand the hesitation and reluctance of governments to bind themselves to prescribed courses of action not at the time rendered strictly necessary by pressing circumstances. The utility of international conferences is not, therefore, to be measured solely by their immediate agreements, but largely by the uncontested principles which issue from their discussions; for these indicate the path along which future action is to be expected. The progress of civilization is of course most promoted by accomplished facts, but sometimes almost equally by the irresistible current of public opinion. It is a great victory for any cause to be able to affirm that the fundamental principles upon which it rests are no longer openly contested.

There was a time, when it was considered by the wisest statesmen that absolute unity of religious belief was necessary to the peace and safety of the State; and fierce wars of religion were fought with that conviction. It was a great triumph for civilization, therefore, when it was established by experience, and could no longer be disputed, that this conviction was erroneous; and that men of the most divergent religious beliefs could not only live in mutual toleration side by side, but unite in equally efficient and loyal support of the same government as their common protector.

THE LIMITATION OF THE EMPLOYMENT OF ARMED FORCE

But united official action, recorded in a solemn convention, has already gone beyond the point of admitting the principle that the Modern State is a justiciable person, whose duty it is to appeal to an international tribunal before resorting to the use of force. This principle was accepted in the discussions of the Second Hague Conference concerning the Limitation of the Employment of Force in the Collection of Contract Debts, and in the Convention itself. The text of this Convention is of such importance that the first article should here be cited in full. It is as follows: —

"The contracting Powers agree not to have recourse to armed force for the recovery of contract debts claimed from the government of one country by the government of another country as being due to its nationals.

This undertaking is, however, not applicable when the debtor State refuses or neglects to reply to an offer of arbitration, or after accepting the offer, prevents any *compromis* from being agreed on, or, after the arbitration, fails to submit to the award." [1]

What then are the logical implications of this agreement with regard to the "right" of war? First, it implies, that a State should be treated as inviolable, provided it admits that it is justiciable. Second, that it is the duty of a State to admit that it is justiciable, even when only the right of a private individual is involved. And, third, that the traditional "right" of war should be so limited as to apply only where there is a denial of justice.

[1] *La Deuxième Conférence Internationale de la Paix*, 1907, Actes et Documents I; and Scott, *The Hague Peace Conferences*, II, pp. 357, 358.

It is evident that this Convention marks one of the most decided steps in advance in the development of International Law that have ever been taken by a single action. It effectually disposes of all the theoretical objections which have from time to time been raised against the possibility of adjusting international differences by judicial methods. The great significance of it is apparent, when we consider, that, until it was negotiated, the right was claimed to overpower a debtor nation by force and to occupy its territory until the demands of the creditor were satisfied, and perhaps in permanence, without any judicial determination of the reality of the obligation, or of the amount of the alleged indebtedness. The way was, therefore, open for the most flagrant forms of injustice, under the nominal sanction of International Law.

Undoubtedly, it is unscrupulous for a debtor government to repudiate its debts, involving the impoverishment of honest people who — perhaps imprudently — invested their savings in securities based on its promises; but what is to be said of the use of armies and navies to enforce upon defenceless populations the payment of purely fictitious claims? A Modern State should recoil with shame and horror from demanding at the cannon's mouth millions where only thousands were justly due, or where there was no just claim whatever; and yet, in one instance where arbitration was employed, claimants demanded more than eight million dollars, but the international commission that adjudicated the claims, after hearing the evidence, allowed only about six hundred thousand;[1] and, in another notable case, less than one-tenth of the amount claimed was allowed.[2]

[1] Ralston, *Report on the Venezuela Claims*, Washington, 1906.
[2] Darby, *Modern Pacific Settlements*, p. 143.

When it is considered that such disputes — having on the one side a superficial aspect of redressing a wrong in behalf of an injured claimant, and yet on the other arousing the most just indignation of the falsely accused debtor — are peculiarly fitted to produce far-reaching political complications, especially where the interests of several nations are involved, we perceive the incalculable advantage of being able to refer all cases of this kind to a properly constituted court for adjudication.

THE ESTABLISHMENT OF INTERNATIONAL COURTS

It is not, therefore, surprising that, at the Second Hague Conference, an immense interest was displayed in the establishment not only of an International Prize Court, to settle questions of maritime capture in time of war, but of a Permanent Court of Arbitral Justice, to which differences of another character might be promptly referred in time of peace. The convention for the formation of the Prize Court was successfully negotiated, and adopted by the Conference; but the convention for the proposed Court of Arbitral Justice had a less happy fate. As the subject of establishing it in another way is at present a matter of official negotiation, it is not expedient to discuss it here; but it may not be improper to say, that the plan proposed was elaborated by jurists of the highest authority, that both in conception and form it met with general approval, and failed of adoption only because of the difficulty of meeting the wishes of all the States regarding the appointment of judges. The most notable fact in connection with this subject was the general conviction that the methods of jurisprudence, rather than the methods of diplomacy, should characterize an international court;

or, in other words, that justice rather than compromise should be the standard of judgment to be applied.

It cannot be doubted that international diplomacy is destined to play a larger rôle in the relations of Sovereign States than it has played hitherto; for these relations demand a continuity of attention that is indispensable, and with the widening of international interests, now embracing the entire globe, the knowledge required of the diplomatist and the objects upon which it must be exercised are immeasurably more extended than they ever have been in the past. The task of the diplomatist will, therefore, grow instead of diminishing; but its character will be different. It will henceforth have in it less of intrigue, and a higher regard for juristic principles. The existence of an international court will in no respect lessen the work of diplomacy, whose main object will be so to transact international business as to keep out of court; just as the trustee of a great fiduciary interest or any intelligent business man will endeavor so to manage his affairs as to avoid litigation.

All the more, therefore, should the international court be based on jurisprudence, and not on diplomacy; partly for the reason that diplomacy will have already done its work before a case will be referred to the court, which is, therefore, needed to do what diplomacy has not been able to accomplish; but partly, also, in order to fix the standard according to which diplomacy must perform its task, knowing that the court stands there to show, that, if its work be not done in a spirit of fairness, its pretensions will not be sustained.

THE DEMANDS FOR INTERNATIONAL JUSTICE FROM THE BUSINESS WORLD

With the enormous extension of international trade and the creation of international industries, the need for justice between private persons and foreign governments is becoming almost as pressing as that for justice between different States. This was strongly felt in the preparation of the project for the International Prize Court. Hitherto, questions of maritime prize have been decided by municipal courts; but the disadvantages of that method are too obvious to mention. Under the fourth article of the Prize Court Convention, it is provided, that appeal to the Court may be made by a neutral individual, if the judgment of the National Court injuriously affects his property; and, under certain conditions, even by an individual subject or citizen of an enemy Power.

But the Court of Prize, being confined to cases arising in time of war, is of far less importance than a Court of Arbitral Justice, designed for the greater number and variety of cases liable to occur in time of peace. The improvements in rapid transportation and communication of intelligence have converted the whole world into one vast market-place. Along with the growth of international commerce has come the growth of international credit. All the great merchants, all the great bankers, and many of the great manufacturers — not to mention the great lines of oversea transportation — have become, or are becoming, international. In time of need, the banks of Paris come to the help of those of London, and those of Berlin to the help of those of New York, without regard to political relations. Capital knows no country; and, answering to its call, labor quickly follows it. All these great enterprises speak for peace, and are far more desirous to have the protection of courts than that of armies and navies.

In proportion as a business community finds its interests acquiring an international character, it becomes aware of the importance of international justice; and seeks for better guarantees, that it may be sure of obtaining it. In a recent article of unusual interest, the late Dr. Richard Freund, of Berlin, offers a well-reasoned plea for an International Arbitral Court for the settlement of differences between private persons and foreign States. "It is not surprising," he says, "that the questions of international economic intercourse become more and more prominent each year, and that ever new, and formerly unsuspected, problems in this province confront International Law; . . . which, in earlier times, was merely an adjunct of politics, but is on the point of being transformed into the law of international intercourse." [1]

"Whereas," he continues, "up to a short time ago, there was little interest manifested in Germany for this colossal development, . . . it seems as though this were to be different now, considering that more lively interest in the construction of the law of international intercourse is being shown. . . . In a memorial addressed by the Eldest of the Merchants' Association of Berlin to the Imperial Chancellor, on the subject of the establishment of an international court of arbitration for disputes between private persons and foreign countries, the wretched insufficiency of the present legal status in this respect is drastically depicted, and reference made to prominent authorities." [2]

The desirability of attaching this additional function to the

[1] *Der Tag*, Berlin, Dec. 8, 1910.
[2] *Correspondenz der Aeltesten der Kaufmannschaft von Berlin*, Oct. 31 1910.

Permanent Tribunal at The Hague has been supported by a number of respected experts in Germany, and a precedent for it is cited in the provisions just referred to in the Convention for the International Court of Prize.

SUMMARY AND CONCLUSION

We are now approaching the end of the task we have undertaken, namely, to throw some light upon the problem of world organization, considered in its juristic sense, as affected by the nature of the Modern State.

The line of thought we have followed has been intended to show the peculiar adaptability of the Modern State for entering into a world organization in the juristic sense. We have seen that it is preeminently an embodiment of law; that it is a juristic person, possessing rights and obligations; that its functions as a promoter of the general welfare involve no impairment of its juristic character; that it is a member of a society of juridical equals; that it is a subject of positive laws, freely accepted; that it is the mediator of guarantees designed to preserve the peace and safety of the society of States; that, even as an armed power, entitled to employ force for its defence and for the maintenance of its rights, it is subject to regulations for the exercise of that power; and, finally, that, without derogation from its autonomy and independence, it is juridically answerable for its conduct, in accordance with the principles of justice.

We have seen also, that the groundwork for the judicial organization of peace has been already far more completely laid than, even two decades ago, would have appeared possible; and the utility of the provisions made has been demonstrated by experience. These provisions include: (1) a general agreement of the Powers "to use their best efforts to insure the pacific settlement of international differences"; (2) an agreement commending the "good offices or mediation of one or more friendly Powers" for the prevention or termination of war, successfully resorted to in the Conference of Portsmouth, at which the peace between Russia and Japan was concluded; (3) an agreement recommending international commissions of inquiry, resorted to with success in the North Sea incident, when Russian warships, under mistaken impressions, fired upon British fishing vessels; and (4) the recognition of international arbitration as "the most effective, and at the same time the most equitable, means of settling disputes which diplomacy has failed to settle," when these relate to questions of a legal nature or the interpretation of treaties.

In conformity with the principles thus solemnly agreed upon, the contracting Powers have undertaken to maintain the Permanent Tribunal of Arbitration, accessible at all times, provided with a bureau which serves as a registry under the supervision of a Permanent Administrative Council, and furnished with an elaborate code of procedure. In addition to this, through the generosity of a distinguished philanthropist, a suitable building for the accommodation of the Permanent Tribunal is approaching completion at The Hague.

It might seem, therefore, as if the judicial organization of peace had already been substantially accomplished. In principle, it has been; but not in fact. The keystone to the nearly completed arch is still wanting. Every agreement and recommendation contained in the provisions just referred to is qualified by the expression, "as far as circumstances may allow"; which leaves the whole structure to be treated, according to the preference of each signatory, either as a solid reality or as a mere creation in the land of dreams.

And yet but one sentence is necessary to solve the whole problem of world organization, namely: A mutual guarantee, on the part of Sovereign States, that they will not resort to force against one another, so long as the resources of justice contained in these conventions have not been exhausted.

Will such a guarantee ever be given? That is a question for governments to answer. We are here engaged in a purely scientific inquiry, and are not called upon to propose public policies, or to venture upon private prophecy. We may, however, conclude, as the result of our study, that the development of the Modern State has greatly facilitated the mutual understanding of the nations, and has both deepened and enlarged their sense of community. This process is not yet ended, and its final results are not at this time demonstrable; but, if we may estimate the future by the transformations of the last three hundred years, we may reasonably entertain the hope that the energies of mankind may be more and more diverted from plans and preparations for mutual destruction, and devoted to united helpfulness in overcoming vice, misery, disease, and ignorance, — the common enemies of man.

INDEX

Absolutism, Machiavelli's theory of, 17–19; not possessed by the people, 18; Bodin tried to vindicate, 24; growth of, 94–95; burden of, intolerable, 96

Achaean League a feeble alliance, 72

Advantages *in posse*, Dangers arising from, 64–65

Age of Absolutism, The, 94–95, 96

Aix-la-Chapelle, International Law recognized in declaration of, 122

Alabama Claims, The, 191

Alexander I and the "Holy Alliance," 145

Alien, The, without rights, in primitive times, 83–85

Althusian postulate of inherent rights, 27–30

Althusius, Johann, on sovereignty as a right inherent in the body politic, 22–23; the true conception of the State, 24; presupposed a natural moral order, 27

Amphictyonic League a religious fraternity, 72

Anarchy, Condition of international, 15

Arbitral Justice, A permanent Court of, 162; defeated at Second Hague Conference, 195; importance of, 197–99

Arbitration, Discussion on, at First Hague Conference, 161; great advance of, 163, 100 02; compulsory, 191–92; a Permanent Tribunal of, agreed upon, 200

Arbitration, International, recognized, 200

Arguments, based on practices and convictions only, worthless, 177

Armaments, National defence the plea for, 13; tendency of the passion for, 13; reason for dreading growth of, 14; the movement for limiting, 156–59; economic burdens imposed by, 157; First Committee on limitation of, reported proposals for humanizing war, 159; Second Committee occupied itself with laws and customs of war, 159; overgrowth of, a constant menace, 166

Armed force, Limitation of employment of, 193–95

Armed peace of Europe, Heavy expenses caused by the, 156–57, 158–59

Art, science, and industry, Development of, under the State, 104–7; under patronage of princes, 107; outward signs of civilization, 108

Assyria a dominion of force, 71

Austin, John, denies International Law in a jural sense, 120

Authority, Universal, defeated, 3

Avignon, Transfer of Papal throne to, 80

Ayala, Balthazar, recognized a society of States governed by law, 82

Baker, Sir Sherston, on the obligation of a State to render justice, 186

Balance and coördination in the relations of life, 30

Balloons, Throwing projectiles and explosives from, 168

Barbeyrac, Jean, the Naturalist, 112

Belgium made neutral territory, 142

Bentham, Jeremy, gave name to *Inter*national Law, 112

Bluntschli, Professor, prepared a "Modernes Völkerrecht," 123; von Moltke's letter to, on war, 153

INDEX

Bodin, Jean, Conception of sovereignty of, 19–22; "De la République" of, 20; the foundation of subsequent political thought, 21; places the State in category of Might not Right, 22, 182; failed to place State in the order of juristic thought, 22; tried to vindicate absolutism, 24

Bombardment by naval forces in time of war, 126, 168

Boniface VIII, Controversies of, with national monarchs, 80

British Association for the Promotion of Social Science, Committee of, appointed to prepare an international code, 123

Brotherhood, Sense of universal, in Middle Ages, 79–80

Burlamaqui, Jean Jacques, the Naturalist, 112

Business world, Demands from the, for international justice, 197–99

Bynkershoek, Cornelius van, found International Law in the treaties between States, 113

Caracalla accorded right of citizenship, 86

Central administration, Obstacles to, 3

Charles the Great ordained roof, fire and water, for the stranger, 86

Chigi, papal nuncio at Osnabrück, 94

China, Awakening of jural consciousness in, 149–50

Christendom, a self-conscious community, 77, 78; sense of unity throughout, 80; permanently divided, 80

Church, The, and the Empire, 16; unifying influences of, 78–80

Civil Law the *Jus Civile* of the Romans, 31

Civilization, Long course of development of, 2; proceeds by refluent movements, 24–25; derived from influence of Roman Empire, 77–78; what is, 104–7; due to protection of the State, 106; the State the measure of, 107–9; the extent of the juristic idea, 108; essential unity of, 109–11; error in speaking of, 109–10; a process of development, 110; ideals precious to, preserved by national independence, 138; rôle of force in, 154–56

Civitas Maxima of Wolf, 116

Claims, Fictitious, rejected by arbitration, 194–95

Codification of International Law, Proposed, 123–25

Colonization and trade, Advance of, 11

Communication and transportation, State may manage, 54

Communities, Interrelation of, 42; jural laws formulated for, 43; rights of other, overlooked, 59

Community of nations, A natural, perceived, 80; Suarez on, 81–83

"Compensations," Pernicious doctrine of, and its evils, 134

"Concert of Europe," The, 140–41

Congress, The Second Hague Conference the first universal, in history of the world, 164

Congress of Vienna, The, 144; neither nationality nor rights of peoples considered in, 145

Congress represents the sovereignty of the nation, 189

Consent of nations a foundation for law, 82

Consent of the governed the foundation of a government, 98

Constitution, Government derives authority from a, 97

Constitution of the United States, Rights of a wronged citizen under the, 188–89

Constitutional movement, Opposition to the, 145–46

Contractual debts not to be collected by force, 162

Counsels of perfection Pufendorf's idea of International Law, 43

Court of Arbitral Justice, *see* Arbitral Justice

Court of Claims established, 190

Cross, Power of the sign of the, 78

Cuba, The United States in, 141

Culture, Different forms of, 109; valuable types of, too useful to be lost, 138

Customs created laws, 33–34, 42, 113

INDEX

Defence of national interests, 57–59
Development of a national conscience, 59–61
Diplomacy, The function of, 62–64, 119–20; classic maxims of, 69–72; a dogma of, 74; rôle of jurisprudence in, 117–20; at First Hague Conference, 160–61; the future of international, 196
Distrust, Mutual, keeps nations in arms, 154, 165; augmenting, 157; restrained action at The Hague, 159; a common enemy, 174
Divine prerogative obsolete, 12
Droit d'aubaine, 88–89
Droit d'émigration, 88–89
Droit de détraction, 88
"Dual Alliance" balanced by the "Triple Alliance," to advantage of the smaller States, 132
Dutch Republic, The, 94
Dynastic interest the primal cause of the State, 16–17

Education, State may support and direct, 53–54; development of, under protection of the State, 104–7
Egoism, Alleged essential, of the State, 67–69
Empire, Roman idea of universal, 2–4; the Church and the, 16
England profited by deadlock of continental powers, 132; legal reforms of Henry II in, 176
Equilibrium, international, Guarantees of, 131–32; useful for the smaller States, 132; inadequacy of the system of, 133–35; a purely mechanical conception, 133; bases friendship on the common fear of hostility, 133–34, 135; gave rise to pernicious doctrine of "compensations," 134; disregards international justice, 135
Equilibrium and equity, 29
Europe, The national units of, how formed, 17; lowest state of degradation in, 91
Evolution, The problem of general social, from the point of view of jurisprudence, 2

Evolution, Contemporary, of International Law, 125–27

Fear and distrust, 70–71; linger on, 73; the ground for general, 74; caused by treaties of alliance, 130–31
Federation, The principle of, 135–39; rests on the assumption of amity, 135; great example of, the American Union, 135–36; the present German Empire, 136–37; extension of juristic relations by, 137; impediments to general, 138–39
Feudal system, The, 16
Field, David Dudley, prepared "Draft outlines of an international code," 123
Fiori's "Il Diretto Internazionale Codificato," 123
Force, organized, Achievements of, under law, 10–12, 166; arbitrary use of, a menace, 58, 166; the rôle of, in civilization, 154–56; secret organization of, perilous, 166; a menace to the State, 167
France, Rule of, on neutral property on enemy's ships, 34
Frederick the Great as writer and statesman, 45
Freund, Dr. Richard, Plea of, for an International Arbitral Court, 198
Function of diplomacy, 62–64

Garden, Count de, the great pedagogue of diplomacy, 70
Geneva Convention, Adaptation of the principles of the, to naval war, 126
Gentilis, Albericus, discerned law in the consent of nations, 82
Germanic race, Characteristics of the, 86–87
Government, A, consists of persons acting in the name of a State, 55–56; form of, not essential, 56; may not be used for predatory purposes, 57; should protect the real interests of its State, 57–58; as the curator of the State, 61–62; reluctant to take precautions, 65; acceptance by, of the juristic char-

Government, A, *continued*,
acter of the State needed, 75;
equal recognition of all forms of,
93–94; influence of new theories
of, upon the Society of States,
95–98; for defence of rights, 97;
by consent of the governed, 98;
mandate of man to his, 101–2
Government, arbitrary, Claims of
divine prerogative for, 12
Grand Duchy of Moscovy, The, 94
Grand Monarch, The Age, of the, 95
Great Britain, Right of, to determine rules of the sea, 187
Great Powers, The united action of
the, a failure, 146; conflicting interests of the, 172; do not desire
war, 174
Greek city-states, The, 2
Grotius constructed the science of
universal jurisprudence, 23–24;
pointed out the higher and universal sovereignty, 24; presupposed a
natural moral order, 27; idea of
of law imposed by nature, 30–33,
110; reclassifies law, 31; gives
proofs for Natural Law, 32; influential part of work of, 32; faith
of, in the moral element of Natural
Law, 33; first great apostle of, 34,
110; on a standard of right, 60; on
the brutal struggle among nations,
92–93; the adherents of 113–15;
fertility of the method of, 114–15
Guarantees, The State as a mediator
of, 130–50; of international equilibrium, 131–32; the principle of
federation, 135–39
Guarantees of justice, Need of, 74–76

Hague Conferences, The, have made
all Powers equal, 122; definite code
adopted by, 126; the First
a "Peace Congress," 158; Convention on Limitation of Armed Force
at Second, 193–94. *See also* International Conference
Hall, William Edward, on International Law and war, 179–80
Hanseatic Cities, The, 94
Hatred and hostility, The illusion of,
74

Henry II, Legal reforms of, 176
Hobbes, Thomas, on the State 37;
on spoliation as a trade, 89; on
nations in perpetual war, 91–92;
crude materialism in philosophy of,
95–96
Holland saved by appeal to principle
of equilibrium, 132
Holy Alliance, The, for reactionary
policies, 145; failure of, 145–46;
effacement of national sovereignty
by, 148–49
Holy Roman Empire, The, 94
Honor of a State, The, 65–67
Hospitality of the Germans, 86
Hospitium among the Romans, 85–86
Hostilities, Code regarding the opening of, 126, 168
House of Austria, Smaller States
saved by combination against, 132
House of Bourbon, Smaller States
saved by combination against, 132
Human interests, Solidarity of all, 3

Ideals, National independence necessary to preservation and development of, 138
Ihering, Rudolf von, "Der Kampf
ums Recht" of, 151
Imperial idea, Postulates of the, 3;
failure and abandonment of the,
3; more than compensated for, 8
Independence, Spirit of local, 3
Independent States, The jural relations of, 144–46
Individual, The, in relation to nature
and his kind, 4; rights and duties
of, 5; inherent rights of, 184
Inherent rights, Althusian postulate
of, 27–30; sovereign power based
on, 98–100; the idea of, 184
Injustice for sake of the State, 45–46
Innocent X protested against the
treaties of peace, 94
Innocent, Immunity of the, 184–85
Institut de Droit International
founded, 123–24
Interdependence between States develops rights of the nature of public duties, 140
Interest, an advantage *in posse*,
62

INDEX

Interests of individuals, protected by the State, 56–57; Hobbes's theory of, 95–96

Interests of the body politic, 61; Hobbes on, 96

International arbitration, Recognition of, 200

International commissions of inquiry agreed upon, 200

International Conference at The Hague, The First, conducted as a "Peace Congress," 158; attitude toward international justice in, 159–62; First Committee discussed proposals for humanizing war, 159; Second Committee the laws and customs of war, 159; Third Committee gave the Conference a quasi-juristic character, and saved it from failure, 159–60; framed a convention for the peaceful settlement of international difficulties, 160; subordinated justice to peace, 161–62

International Conference at The Hague, The Second, 162–65; the programme, 162; increased interest in the juristic idea at, 162–63; limitation of employment of armed force by, 193–94

International conferences, Measure of utility of, 192

International court for maritime prizes, 162, 168, 195, 197

International courts, Establishment of, 195–96

International guarantees, The limit and basis of, 148–50; based on juristic character of the Modern State, 149–50

International intervention and supervision, 140–41

International Jurisprudence. Grotius constructed the science of, 23–24; mere ideology to many, 71; principles of, a basis for positive rights, 111; opposition of "naturalists" and "positivists," 111–13; contribution of Wolf to, 115–17; rôle of, in diplomacy, 117–20

International justice, Attitude toward, in the First Hague Conference, 159–62; the progress of, 190–93; demands for, from the business world, 197–99

International Law, Defined by Pufendorf, 43–44; development of, along the general plan laid down by Grotius, 113–15; Vattel's contribution to positive, 117–19; nature and authority of, 120–22; explicitly recognized, 122; proposed codification of, 123–25; evolution of, 125–27; subjection of the State to the reign of, 127–29; no obstacle to submission of the Modern State to, 128–29

International Law Association, The, established, 123

International relations, Application of rules to peaceful, 126–27; the element of danger in, 155–56

International rights and duties, Uncontested juristic character of, 192

International society, States members of an, 77; import of Locke's theory for an, 100–2

Interpretation of moral law, Necessity of a correct, 45–47

Intervention and supervision, International, 140–41

Inviolability, The principle of, 184–86; should be established in the Law of Nations, 185

Italian city-states, Principle of equilibrium guaranteed existence of, 132

Italy dismembered requires tyranny of Borgia, 18

Judicial organization of peace, 169–71

Jural conceptions built up by the nations for themselves, 8

Jural consciousness, The, of each separate State, 9; wide-spread new element in the Modern State, 72–73; of nations developing, 82; awakening of, in Russia, Persia, Turkey, and China, 149–50

Jural equality of States in an international society, 77

Jural guarantees, Adaptability of the Modern State for, 146–48

Jural law, Prevalence of, 10; formulated for communities, 42–43; mandate of man regarding, 102–3; narrow conception of, 120; defined, 121; recognition of, 128

Jural laws, rules of action enforced by public authority, 7–8; the security for human rights, 9

Jural relations of independent States, 144–46

Jural rights possessed by every one, 28

Jural unity of all civilized States, 116

Jurisprudence, international, based on custom, Serious impediment to, 34

Jurisprudence, Universal, *see* International Jurisprudence, International Law, Law of Nations

Juristic character alone confers supreme authority on the State, 54–55

Juristic conception of the State, Progress toward the, in First and Second Hague Conferences, 160–63; no objection raised to, in principle, 163; not yet organized, 164–65; only recently recognized, 187

Juristic entity, Duties of the State as a, 65–67, 69–70

Juristic idea applied by Grotius to international relationships, 23; considerable gains for the, 24; in the State, 107; triumph of the, in 1907, 162–63, 164

Juristic ideals, The highest fulfilment of, the real strength of a State, 54–55

Juristic order, Place of the State in the, 22–25, 55; ultimate creation of a positive, 117

Juristic person, The State as a, 26–52; what is the honor of a, 66

Juristic progress, Grotius bases the principle of, on the Law of Nations, 31

Jus Civile, the law of Rome, 31

Jus Gentium derived from *Jus Naturae* 30, 31; 112

Jus inter Gentes of Zouch, 112

Jus Naturae, the primary source of *Jus Gentium*, 30; inherent in the whole human race, 31

Justice, No human cosmos without, 29; the sort of, that finds a place in public morals, 50; between nations, 60; need of guarantees of, 74–76; a living power, 151; the imperfect organization of, the menace to public peace, 155–56; the path of, the only sure path to peace, 156; will destroy Mutual Distrust, 174; evolution of organized, 175–77

Justinian on the people as the origin of law-making power, 18; on *Jus Naturae*, 31

Law, The State as an embodiment of, 1–25; early aspirations for reign of, 2–4; supremacy of, based upon reason, 3; obstacles to uniform, 3; inherent in society, 4–5; a necessity of the nature and social needs of men, 4; the concept of, 5; pretension of supremacy to, 13–14; sovereignty of, the only true sovereignty, 24; the Natural and Voluntary of Grotius, 31–33; as distinguished from morality, 121

Law of Nations, Grotius developed the, 23–24, 110; the sum of principles and practice in use, 31; identified with Law of Nature by Pufendorf, 34–35, 110–11; the "Positivists" and the, 112–13; influence of "dictates of right reason" in determining a positive, 114–15; sovereigns of Europe pledged to the observance of the principles of, 122;

Law of Nature, The, inherent in the reason of man, 23; of the Stoics, 30; and the Law of Nations, of Grotius, 31; the dictates of right reason, 31; a corrective of the customs of nations, 33–34; the "Naturalists" and, 111–12, 114; the "Positivists" and, 113–15.

Law, positive, The State as a subject of, 103–29

Lawlessness, the menace to public peace, 155–56

Law-making power, The people the, 18

INDEX

Laws, Natural, moral, and jural, 5–8; natural, the phenomena of nature, 6; moral, directions for conduct, 6–7; jural, rules of action enforced by public authority, 7–8

Laws that should be observed even in time of war not silent, 23; or rights, which first, 28

Leaders, Passions and ambitions of, 3

Legal obligation, A starting point for the idea of, 22

"Leviathan," The State called, by Hobbes, 37

Lincoln and emancipation, 46

Literature and education, Development of, under the State, 104–7; under patronage of princes, 107

Locke, John, Theory of government of, 97–102; for the defence of rights, 97; based on consent of the governed, 98; effect of, on conception of sovereignty, 98–100; import of, for international society, 100–2

Luxemburg made neutral territory, 142

Lytton, Lord, on difference between State and individual, 48; on the kind of justice that has a place in public morals, 50; condemned by the ballot-boxes, 51

Machiavelli, Theory of absolutism of, 17–19; contribution of, to political science, 18; the Prince the State for, 18–19, 26; philosophy of, the classic of European statesmanship, 19–20; fundamental error of, 19; Grotius the great adversary of, 24; theory of the State of, 26–27, 43; rights the progeny of law, 28; untenable theory of, 28–30; Frederick the Great wrote against teachings of, 45

Magna Charta, A, for the society of European States, 94

Majestas, 21

Man, Mandate of, to his governments, 102–3

Man and society at war, 33

Mankind, The essential unity of, 3

Maritime law, affirmed in declaration of Paris, 122

Maritime welfare, Rules of, the oldest in law international, 34; declaration of the Conference of London regarding, 126, 168; right of capture in, 168

Martens, George Friedrich von, "Recueil des Traités" of, 113

Medea a dominion of force, 71

Mediation or good offices of friendly Powers agreed upon, 200

Mediterranean, The ancient sea-laws of the, on neutral property on enemy's ships, 34; commercial nations of the, based on wealth, 72

Merchant ships, Conversion of, into warships, 126, 168; status of enemy, at outbreak of hostilities, 126 168

Merchants' Association of Berlin, Memorial by the Eldest of, for an international court of arbitration, 198

Metternich, Masterly activity of, 146

Middle Ages, Society under two forms in the, 16; that every one has rights recognized in the, 90

Might makes right, Bodin's doctrine that, 22, 182

Military purposes, Excessive expense for, 13

Military virtue, The value of, 152–54

Modern State, *see* State, and State, Modern

Molé, Mathieu, on the Peace of Westphalia, 94

Moltke, Count von, on war and peace, 153–54

Monarchies, national, Rise of, 16–17; France and Spain successful, 18

Moral delinquency, Judgment of a, must consider all circumstances, 46–47; often a choice of alternatives, 46–47

Moral law, The, vindicates itself, 38–39; relation of the State to, 38–42; applies to nations and to states, 39; inadequacy of, for the State, 42–44; alleged exemption of State from, 44–45; the necessary interpretation of, 45–47

Moral laws, directions for conduct, 6–7

P

Moral order, A natural, 27–30
Morality, Public and private, 49–52
Moser, Johann Jakob, on International Law, 113
Münster, Treaties of peace signed at, 93

Napoleon I, Coalition to overthrow, 144; legal and judicial reforms instituted by, 176
National conscience, Development of a, 59–61
National defence, The, everywhere the plea for armament, 13; a specific obligation assumed by the State, 13
National independence necessary to preservation and development of ideals, 138–39; limitations of, 139–40
National interests, The defence of, 57–59; many, that are not rights, 62, 63–64; dangers from latter, 64–65
National strength the only measure of national safety, 70
Nations have no body and no soul, That, an error, 49–50
Natural laws, the phenomena of nature, 6
Natural resources, The State may exploit, 54
"Naturalists," The, 111–12, 114
Nature the great law-giver, 4
Nature, The Law of, *see* the Law of Nature
Navies, Development of modern, 11
Neutral powers and persons, Rights and duties of, in case of war on land, 126, 168; rights and duties of, in naval war, 126
Neutral property on enemy's ship, Laws regarding, 34
Neutralization, The principle of, 142–44; of use to the guaranteeing Powers, 143; what guarantees to the greater States, 144
Non-moral form of society, A, not imaginable, 28–30
North Sea incident, The, 200

Obedience, Conflict of temporal with spiritual forms of, 3; power to compel, not a reason for obligation of, 22; authority of State to command, 26
Omnipotence of the State, Danger of the, 12–13, 14
Oppenheim, Dr., on the fanatics of international peace, 178–79; definition of war, 180–81
Osnabrück, Treaties of peace signed at, 93, 94
Ottoman Empire, The, excluded from the Peace of Westphalia, 94
Outlawry of the stranger in primitive times, 83–85

Paris, Declaration of, affirmed existence of maritime law, 122
Paris, Treaty of, admits the Sublime Porte to the advantages of Public Law and of the European Concert. 122
Peace, The effective organization of, 3; the end of justice, attained by conflict, 151; Count von Moltke on, 153–54; the question of, always a question of justice, 164–65; the warlike maintenance of, 165–67; judicial organization of, 169–71; periods of, longer than war periods, 173; groundwork for judicial organization of, laid, 199–200
Peace Congress at The Hague, 158
Peace of Westphalia inspired by the idea of law, 33; The Thirty Years' War and the, 91–93; significance of the, 93–95; Mathieu Molé on the, 94
Permanence in the midst of change, 29
Persia a dominion of force, 71; awakening of jural consciousness in, 149–50
Personality, Rights and duties essential properties of, 5
Philippines, The United States in the, 141
Piracy driven from the seas, 11
Political communities, Undeveloped, 187–88
Politician and his policy, Ruemelin's distinction between the, 47–48
Pope, The, arbiter of quarrels, in the days of faith, 80

INDEX

Popular impulse, Danger from, 65
"Positivists," the, Opposition of "Naturalists" and, 111–13; resort of, to general principles of Naturalist school, 114–15
Possession and obligation, The relation of, 29–30
Power, Supreme, a negative idea, 182
Power upon the sea, The question of, 11
Powers, Agreements entered into by the, 199–200
Predatory warfare become obsolete, 12–13
Prince, Whatever pleases the, has the force of law, 17; the State, for Machiavelli, 18–19, 26–27
Princeps legibus solutus est not a legal maxim, 22
Private International Law, Effort for rules of, 127
Prize Court, *see* International Court
Public morality, A, of moderation and kindly pretence, 50
Public officer, Responsibility of the, 47, 49–52; has no reason to practise falsehood or immorality for benefit of the State, 50; not exempt from rules of private morality, 51
Public policies, Relation of a statesman to the morality of, 47–49; should be in harmony with moral law, 51
Public rights and interests, The realm of conflicting, 128
Public utilities, State may construct and administer, 53
Pufendorf, first great apostle of doctrines of Grotius, 34, 110; identified Law of Nations with Law of Nature, 34–35, 110–11; defined the State as a *moral person*, 35; modern jurists agree with, 37; thought only moral law could be applied to States, 43
Pufendorf's idea of the State as a moral person, 33–36

Races, The disparity of, 3
Rachel, Samuel, on the Law of Nations, 113

Realism in government, Triumph of, 19
Reason, Diversity of the revelations of, 3–4; the guide of practical life in human experience, 4; common to all men, 23; law never abdicates the throne of, 23–24; natural moral order revealed by, 27
Reign of law, Early aspirations for, 2–4
Religion, Cruelties practised in name of, 177
Revolutions a protest against injustice, 54
Right, A, claimed, subversive of all right, 14
Right and wrong, Concepts of, 30
Right of war, The, 178–83; defenders of the, 178–79; no law on, 179–80; fallacy of the absolute, 181–83; reserved to a Sovereign State, 181
Righteous politics, A judgment for, 51
Rights, the foundation of society, 28; asserted in the Law of Nature of the Stoics, 30–31; protection of, the primary purpose of the State, 54; of the individual, 56; of stranger, slowly recognized by the Germanic race, 86–87; government for defence of, 97; security of, under just laws, the stamp of civilization, 108–9; distinction between individual and political, 115–16; and duties of States, 186–87
Robe d'ennemi confisque robe d'ami, 34
Roman conceptions of right, Soundness of the, 9
Roman Empire, Influence of the, 77–78; Church more influential than the, 78; official courts established under the, 176
Roman law, Conquests of, more enduring than those of Roman legions, 8–9, 77–78
Ruemelin, Gustav, on exemption of State from moral law, 44–45; on responsibility of a public officer, 47–48
Russia, Awakening of jural consciousness in, 149–50

INDEX

Russia, Emperor of, Rescript of, on the cost of armaments, 157–58
Rutherford, Thomas, the Naturalist, 112

St. Bartholomew's Day, 20
Salisbury, Lord, on the heavy expenses caused by the armed peace of Europe, 156–57
Schism, The Great, of 1378, 80
Self-consciousness, Development of, in the Society of States, 87–90
Self-interest of the State, 48; becomes patriotism, 49
Sidgwick, Professor, on recognition of rights in the Middle Ages, 90
Social forces becoming interrelated, 2
Social relations of States the function of diplomacy, 62–64
Society, Whole nature of, changed, 73–74
Society of States, Recognition of, by Suarez, 81–83; development of self-consciousness in the, 87–90; existed in a "state of nature," 89–90; a Magna Charta for the, 94; influence of new theories of government upon the, 95–98; capable of jural organization, 100–1; evils existing in the, 101–2; law inherent in the, 116; all autonomous and independent States admitted to the, 122
Souveraineté, 21
Sovereign States of Europe slow to recognize reciprocal jural rights, 87; the Peace of Westphalia a compact between the, 93–94
Sovereign States throughout the world recognize International Law, 122; right of, to declare war, 178–83; all juridically equal, 185–86
Sovereigns, Rise and power of, 16–17; implied by attribute of sovereignty, 21
Sovereignty, a term employed for a double purpose, 14; of the State, 15; transferred from sovereign to State, 17; the essence of the State, 17; Bodin's conception of, 19–22, 182, 183; absolute, indivisible, inalienable, 21; obstacle to placing State in the juristic order of ideas, 21–22; Althusian conception of, as an inherent right, 22–24; the foundation and substance of a State, 23; effect of Locke's doctrine on the conception of, 98–100; a negative idea, 182
Spoliation, International, has ceased to be a trade, 73; Hobbes on, 89
State, The, in Europe and in Africa, 1; nature of the Modern Constitutional, 1–2; polity of the Modern, 4; the embodiment and protagonist of law, 8–10, 74, 147; essentially a local institution, 9; with a jural consciousness, 9; the greatest of human institutions, 10; world organization must be effected by instrumentality of, 10; firmly established the world over, 10; must be entrusted with organized force, 11; danger of omnipotence of, 12–13; attributes of, derived from the people, 12; real peril of the, 13–14; pretension of supremacy to law, 14; sovereignty of, 15; genesis and development of, 15–17; no, in the Middle Ages, 16; evolution of, 16; dynastic interest the primal cause of, 16; sovereignty the essence of, 17; theory of, a mental creation, 18; the creation of the Prince, 18–19; Bodin's abstract theory of, 20–21; placed in category of Might not of Right, 22; place of, in the juristic order, 22–25; sovereignty as a right the foundation and substance of, 23; in category of Right not Might, 23; opposing conceptions of, Machiavellian and Althusian, 24; as a juristic person, 26–52, 99–100; Machiavellian theory of, 26–27; essentially non-moral, 27, 43; such a, cannot be conceived, 28–30; greatest of human institutions, 30; Pufendorf's idea of, as a moral person, 33–36; considered as a person, 36–38; a unit among other units of like kind, 36; can receive and bestow benefits and injuries, 36; personality ascribed to, 37; the jural expression

INDEX 213

State, The — *continued*
of Man the Species, 38; relation of, to moral law, 38–42; cannot avoid effects produced by its acts, 39–40; the formula of morality for, 41–42; inadequacy of the moral law for, 42–44; alleged exemption of, from morality, 44–45; unjust acts in interest of, 46–47; self-interest of, 48; becomes patriotism, 49; as a promoter of general welfare, 53–76; duty of, to its constituents, 53–55; protection of rights the primary purpose of, 54; autonomous, 55; and its government, 55–57; the defence of national interests by, 57–59; should maintain its juristic character, 59, 76; development of a national conscience in, 59–61; government as the curator of, 61–62; an economic entity, 61; duties of, as a juristic entity, 65–67; egoism of, 67–69; struggles in formation of, 67–68; a triumph over opposition to authority of law, 69; essentially a juristic entity, 69–70; passion for plunder of, 70–72; new element in modern, 72–74; need that justice be guaranteed by, 75–76; as a member of a society, 77–103; self-consciousness of, intensified, 94; the creature of rights, 98–100; as a subject of positive law, 103–29; the measure of civilization, 107–9; Wolf's doctrine of inherent rights of, 115–16; Vattel's application of, 117–19; subjection of, to the reign of law, 127–29; reverence asked of, for principles of right, 129; as a mediator of guarantees, 130–50; principle of neutralization applied to, 142–44; as an armed power, 151–74; as a justiciable person, 175–201; judicial organization within, slow and difficult, 175–77; responsibility of, 100-00, to render justice, 180; subordination of, to judicial principles, 188–90; a Sovereign, not amenable to a suit at law without its own consent, 190; limitation of use of armed force by, 193–95

State, the Modern, Adaptability of, for jural guarantees, 146–48; founded upon them, 146; guarantees within the, 147; international guarantees no encroachment on, 147–48; the principle of inviolability incorporated in the, 184–85; has no right of war, 185–86
States, Body of rules applicable to conduct of, 31; cannot escape penalty for their acts, 39–40; the social relations of, the function of diplomacy, 62–64; should accept the requirements they impose upon their constituents, 67; small, object to absorption by the larger, 138–39; material differences between, 186–87; a mutual guarantee from Sovereign, wanted, 201
Statesman, Relation of a, to the morality of public policies, 47–49
Story, Justice, on rights of a wronged citizen under American and British Constitutions, 188–89
Stranger, Outlawry of the, in primitive times, 83–85; protected by the *proxenoi* in Greece, 84–85; recognition of rights of the, 85–87; protected in the maritime countries, 88; pillaged by the ruler, 88
Suarez, Franciscus, Recognition of a society of States by, 81–83; in advance of his time, 82
Submarine contact mines, Laying of automatic, 126, 168
Supremacy to law, The pretension of, 13–14; subversive of conception of right, 14; meaning of, 182
Swiss Confederation, The, 94
Switzerland made neutral territory, 142

Textor, Johann Wolfgang, on Law of Nations, 113
Thirty Years' War, The, and the Peace of Westphalia, 91–93
Thomasius, Christian, the Naturalist, 112; feared to publish his convictions, 177
Torture as a method of legal procedure, 176
Trade and colonization, Advance of, 11

INDEX

Treaties of alliance excite alarm, 130–31
Treaty of Chaumont, Renewal of obligations of, 145
"Triple Alliance" balanced by the "Dual Alliance," 132
Turkey, Awakening of jural consciousness in, 149–50

Unifying influences of the Church, 78–80
Union for Railway Transportation, 127
Union for the Protection of Industrial Property, 127
Union for the Protection of Works of Literature and Art, 127
Union for the Publication of Customs Tariffs, 127
Universal Postal Union established, 127
Universal Telegraphic Union established, 127

Vattel, Emerich de, Contribution of, to positive International Law, 117–19
Venetian Oligarchy, The, 93
Verbandsrecht, original conception of law among the Germanic tribes, 86
Voluntary Law includes divine and human, 31

Walker, Professor, on treatment of the stranger, 88

War, Laws that should be observed even in time of, 23; to be right must be just, 34; the call to, 152; von Moltke's apology for, 153–54; peaceful regulation of, 167–69; brings only a temporary settlement, 170; profit and loss in, 172–73; is war inevitable? 173–74; the right of, 178–81; fallacy of, 181–83
War on land, Code of laws and customs of, 126, 168
Warfare, Modern, 170–71
Wars of Religion, The, 20, 192–93
Welfare, The State as promoter of general, 53–76; universal, does not diminish local, 75
Witchcraft, Prosecutions for, 177
Wolf, Christian, Conception of a world-state of, 115–17
World organization, Meaning of, 1; problem of, 2, 22; impossible in juristic sense, if State is absolute, 21–22; why still an unsolved problem, 24; summary and conclusion of arguments for, and progress towards, 199–201
World-State, Wolf's conception of a, 115–17

Zouch, Richard, founder of the Positivist school, 112–13; found law in the customs of nations, 113

C. ALEX. NELSON.

THE COLUMBIA UNIVERSITY PRESS
Columbia University in the City of New York

The Press was incorporated June 8, 1893, to promote the publication of the results of original research. It is a private corporation, related directly to Columbia University by the provisions that its Trustees shall be officers of the University and that the President of Columbia University shall be President of the Press.

The publications of the Columbia University Press include works on Biography, History, Economics, Education, Philosophy, Linguistics, and Literature, and the following series:

Columbia University Biological Series.
Columbia University Studies in Classical Philology.
Columbia University Studies in Comparative Literature.
Columbia University Studies in English.
Columbia University Geological Series.
Columbia University Germanic Studies.
Columbia University Indo-Iranian Series.
Columbia University Contributions to Oriental History and Philology.
Columbia University Oriental Studies.
Columbia University Studies in Romance Philology and Literature.

    Blumenthal Lectures.   Hewitt Lectures.
    Carpentier Lectures.   Jesup Lectures.
    Julius Beer Lectures.

Catalogues will be sent free on application.

LEMCKE & BUECHNER, Agents
30–32 West 27th Street, New York

THE COLUMBIA UNIVERSITY PRESS
Columbia University in the City of New York

LECTURES ON SCIENCE, PHILOSOPHY, AND ART

A SERIES of twenty-one lectures descriptive in non-technical language of the achievements in Science, Philosophy, and Art, and indicating the present status of these subjects as concepts of human knowledge, were delivered at Columbia University, during the academic year 1907–1908, by various professors chosen to represent the several departments of instruction.

MATHEMATICS — By CASSIUS JACKSON KEYSER, Adrain Professor of Mathematics.
PHYSICS — By ERNEST FOX NICHOLS, Professor of Experimental Physics.
ASTRONOMY — By HAROLD JACOBY, Rutherfurd Professor of Astronomy.
GEOLOGY — By JAMES FURMAN KEMP, Professor of Geology.
BIOLOGY — By EDMUND B. WILSON, Professor of Zoölogy.
PHYSIOLOGY — By FREDERIC S. LEE, Professor of Physiology.
BOTANY — By HERBERT MAULE RICHARDS, Professor of Botany.
ZOÖLOGY — By HENRY E. CRAMPTON, Professor of Zoölogy.
ANTHROPOLOGY — By FRANZ BOAS, Professor of Anthropology.
ARCHAEOLOGY — By JAMES RIGNALL WHEELER, Professor of Greek Archaeology and Art.
HISTORY — By JAMES HARVEY ROBINSON, Professor of History.
ECONOMICS — By HENRY ROGERS SEAGER, Professor of Political Economy.
POLITICS — By CHARLES A. BEARD, Adjunct Professor of Politics.
JURISPRUDENCE — By MUNROE SMITH, Professor of Roman Law and Comparative Jurisprudence.
SOCIOLOGY — By FRANKLIN HENRY GIDDINGS, Professor of Sociology.
PHILOSOPHY — By NICHOLAS MURRAY BUTLER, President of the University.
PSYCHOLOGY — By ROBERT S. WOODWORTH, Adjunct Professor of Psychology.
METAPHYSICS — By FREDERICK J. E. WOODBRIDGE, Johnsonian Professor of Philosophy.
ETHICS — By JOHN DEWEY, Professor of Philosophy.
PHILOLOGY — By A. V. W. JACKSON, Professor of Indo-Iranian Languages.
LITERATURE — By HARRY THURSTON PECK, Anthon Professor of the Latin Language and Literature.

These lectures are published by the Columbia University Press separately in pamphlet form, at the uniform price of twenty-five cents, by mail twenty-eight cents. Orders will be taken for the separate pamphlets, or for the whole series. Also to be had in one volume, blue cloth, at $5.00 net; by mail, $5.27.

LEMCKE & BUECHNER, AGENTS
30–32 W. 27th ST., NEW YORK

THE COLUMBIA UNIVERSITY PRESS
Columbia University in the City of New York

COLUMBIA UNIVERSITY LECTURES

BLUMENTHAL LECTURES

POLITICAL PROBLEMS OF AMERICAN DEVELOPMENT. By ALBERT SHAW, LL.D., Editor of the *Review of Reviews*. 12mo, cloth, pp. vii + 268. Price, $1.50 *net*.

CONSTITUTIONAL GOVERNMENT IN THE UNITED STATES. By WOODROW WILSON, LL.D., President of Princeton University. 12mo, cloth, pp. vii + 236. Price, $1.50 *net*.

THE PRINCIPLES OF POLITICS FROM THE VIEWPOINT OF THE AMERICAN CITIZEN. By JEREMIAH W. JENKS, LL.D., Professor of Political Economy and Politics in Cornell University. 12mo, cloth, pp. xviii + 187. Price, $1.50 *net*.

THE COST OF OUR NATIONAL GOVERNMENT. By HENRY JONES FORD, Professor of Politics in Princeton University. 12mo, cloth, pp. xv + 144. Price, $1.50 *net*.

THE BUSINESS OF CONGRESS. By HON. SAMUEL W. MCCALL, Member of Congress for Massachusetts. 12mo, cloth. Price, $1.50 *net*.

JULIUS BEER LECTURES

SOCIAL EVOLUTION AND POLITICAL THEORY. By LEONARD T. HOBHOUSE, Professor of Sociology in the University of London. 12mo, cloth. Price, $1.50 *net*.

CARPENTIER LECTURES

THE NATURE AND SOURCES OF THE LAW. By JOHN CHIPMAN GRAY, LL.D., Royall Professor of Law in Harvard University. 12mo, cloth, pp, xii + 332. Price, $1.50 *net*.

WORLD ORGANIZATION AS AFFECTED BY THE NATURE OF THE MODERN STATE. By HON. DAVID JAYNE HILL, American Ambassador to Germany. 12mo, cloth. Price, $1.50 *net*.

LEMCKE & BUECHNER, AGENTS
30-32 West 27th Street, New York

THE COLUMBIA UNIVERSITY PRESS

Columbia University in the City of New York

COLUMBIA UNIVERSITY LECTURES

HEWITT LECTURES

THE PROBLEM OF MONOPOLY. By JOHN BATES CLARK, LL.D., Professor of Political Economy, Columbia Unversity. 12mo, cloth, pp. vi + 128. Price, $1.25 net.

POWER. By CHARLES EDWARD LUCKE, Ph.D., Professor of Mechanical Engineering, Columbia University. 12mo, cloth, pp. 316. Illustrated. Price, $2.00 net.

THE DOCTRINE OF EVOLUTION. Its Basis and Scope. By HENRY EDWARD CRAMPTON, Ph.D., Professor of Zoölogy, Columbia University. 12mo, cloth. Price, $1.50 net.

SOCIAL IDEALS IN MEDIEVAL STORY. By WILLIAM WITHERLE LAWRENCE, Associate Professor of English, Columbia University. 12mo, cloth. Price, $1.50 net.

JESUP LECTURES

LIGHT. By RICHARD C. MACLAURIN, LL.D., Sc.D., President of the Massachusetts Institute of Technology. 12mo, cloth, pp. ix + 251. Portrait and figures. Price, $1.50 net.

LECTURES ON SCIENCE, PHILOSOPHY, AND ART. A series of twenty-one lectures descriptive in non-technical language of the achievements in Science, Philosophy, and Art, and indicating the present status of these subjects as concepts of human knowledge, delivered at Columbia University during the academic year 1907-1908. 8vo, cloth. Price, $5.00 net.

LECTURES ON LITERATURE. A series of eighteen lectures on literary art and on the great literatures of the world, ancient and modern, delivered at Columbia University by Members of the Faculty during the academic year 1909-1910. In one volume, 8vo, cloth, pp. 404. Price, $2.00 net.

LEMCKE & BUECHNER, AGENTS
30-32 West 27th Street, New York

DATE DUE

DARTMOUTH COLLEGE
3 3311 00817 3421